FROM THE HEART TO THE HEARTLAND

Fred Kroner

OTHER BOOKS BY FRED KRONER:

Parkland Perfection 'Be together, not the same' (2016)

'A Saucer Coming To Rest' A Half-Century of the Assembly Hall (2013)

Catching Up, The Official History of the Eastern Illinois Baseball League (2010)

Are You Ready? Jim Sheppard – A career announcing Illinois football and basketball (2007)

Brian Cardinal: Citizen Pain (2001)

Asphalt Celery (1974)

Books (except Asphalt Celery) available for purchase at fredkroner.com.

CONTENTS

ACKNOWLEDGEMENTS

The author extends sincere thanks to Dani Tietz, for her editing and advice, to Colleen Schultz for her proofreading efforts, and to the dozens of colleagues and thousands of coaches and athletes who for decades have been a major part of this story. Whether they are specifically named or not, they will never be forgotten and are why my 50-plus-year career was so memorable, pleasant and successful. Also playing a vital role was Heather Wanninger, from Sweet Lemonade Photography in Mahomet, who graciously donated her time and talents to shoot the front and back cover photos as well as the About the Author picture. And, a special thanks to my wife Emily Kroner for sharing a part of this journey.

-Fred Kroner

FOREWORD

My family moved to East Central Illinois in 2002 from West Lafayette, Ind. As a very young mother, one thing I was not willing to give up was basketball. With a 3-and 1-year-old at home, I became a junior high basketball coach at Franklin Middle School, in Champaign, prior to taking on the junior varsity position, and then varsity position at Blue Ridge High School, in Farmer City, until 2006.

With the Blue Ridge team comprised of seven members, we didn't win a single game in the 2004-2005 season. I sent in my stats to the newspapers, like every other coach, but our team wasn't covered in the newspapers like those we faced.

I vaguely remember being interviewed by Fred Kroner after one of our seven wins during the 2005-06 season, but if I'm being honest, I remember him more from his byline and smile in The News-Gazette than from being interviewed.

When I learned that Fred Kroner was ready to retire from The News-Gazette in 2015, I knew that it was a big deal. And I realized when the editor of The Mahomet Citizen was thinking about moving on, Fred would be the natural fit to fill in at that position.

I wouldn't be real if I didn't tell you that I was nervous

about the possibility. Fred Kroner was an icon to me, someone untouchable, a big deal. His talent is something that many of us strive to realize, and so I didn't know how the publication I owned, the Mahomet Daily, and how my writing would fare in comparison to his.

But the thing I never understood is why there had to be competition between the two entities: they both have something unique to offer to readers. I hoped that my relationship with the new editor, Fred, could be more like a team rather than a foe.

While Fred is the award-winning writer he is, someone who is well-known in communities throughout the state of Illinois, he quickly helped me to realize that there is something more in this world than squelching the competition.

There is friendship.

When you first meet someone, you exchange pleasantries. But Fred asked if he could interview me for an article to be in the Mahomet Citizen within a few weeks of taking his new post.

Let me reiterate this for you: Fred Kroner, the editor of the Mahomet Citizen, which is owned by The News-Gazette, wanted to interview Dani Tietz, the owner, and editor of the Mahomet Daily, which is in direct competition with his publication.

Not only that, but he also bestowed upon me the honor of telling his story in my publication in the 50th year of his writing career.

There are extraordinary things that happen in this life. This gesture told me everything about who Fred Kroner is.

Fred also suggested that we exchange stories each week to help cut down on our workload. As editors of such publications, we take on the responsibility of everything: finding stories, doing all the interviews, writing the stories, taking photographs, designing or maintaining its distribution, fielding emails and concerns.

A 40-hour work week always turns into a 60-plus hour work week, so one article that would take a few hours to produce is such a gift.

Our working relationship soon turned into a partnership when Fred decided to focus on supporting his wife, Emily, as she jumped into her dream of owning a pastry shop, Lucky Moon Pies & More. Putting in those long hours at the Mahomet Citizen was no longer feasible, but Fred still wanted to write.

It's not just because he can string a few sentences together after listening to and regurgitating a series of events; if trained, anyone can do that. But Fred has a rare gift.

He sees people.

I'm not talking about watching a game and seeing the boy who scores the most points.

I'm talking about knowing that there is a human being standing on that court, a human being who has hopes and desires, one who has failed once or twice, one who more than likely had to overcome something and one who is growing.

Just seeing something is the beginning, though. It takes hours, sometimes days and months, to curate a story, to listen to people talk, to try to understand all the pieces and then to craft a story that is raw and real, informative and complete.

To do this once is luck. To do this consistently is magic.

And that's where Fred Kroner lies: magic.

The stories Fred produces derive from something that can't be taught, though. They come from a curiosity that causes him to listen when someone speaks, from an understanding that holds no judgment when someone makes a confession, from the attention that notices patterns or special moments, from an interest in people that makes them feel like they belong.

We all know Fred Kroner. He's the 6'2" guy sitting at the

press table who looks like he played basketball at one point.

But in all the time he showed us the world through the stories he told, he gave something more. Sure, the byline is important. A story on the front page is special. But Fred created a world where he makes people feel like they belong, no matter what.

When I interviewed Fred, I was surprised to learn that his time playing sports was short-lived. When he was the editor of The Citizen, he told me that he liked his role there because he got to write about more than sports.

Of course, after spending 50 years following sports in East Central Illinois, Fred included those highlights in his memoir. But I hope that as you read this, you will also get to know my friend, Fred Kroner.

He is a talented writer. His name has been in the newspaper thousands of times. He's won awards. He is well-known. But he is so much more than just his job.

Fred is a visionary who consistently pushes himself outside of the box, who overcomes obstacles and who makes sure that he is producing something that not only moves the world forward, but also creates a soft place for people to share their triumphs as well as their failures.

He never forgets that there is a person sitting in front of him during an interview. Because of that, he oftentimes ends up walking beside them in the future.

It's a gift that very few people in this world are able to offer.

We have all been blessed by Fred Kroner. And once more, we are blessed to read his story, in his words.

-Dani Tietz

CHAPTER ONE

Welcome to my world.

It is a world that includes many envious people.

"You get paid for covering ball games?"

"What can be better?"

Those comments are not the most frequent ones I hear.

Many of my days include an exchange such as this:

"Fred? Fred Kroner?"

"Yes," I say.

"Well, how are you?"

"Fine," I say."

After enduring this scenario dozens of times each year, I've learned to be proactive.

"I'm sorry," I say. "I can't remember your name."

"Oh, you don't know me," the speaker will invariably respond. "I've seen you at ball games for years and your picture has been in the paper, so I feel like I know you."

That couldn't be further from the truth, which is why this book became a priority.

There's one subject I know more about than anyone else: Myself.

It's time to share.

I've often wondered if my professional career as a newspaper writer was destined.

I was born early on a Wednesday morning in mid-November, 1955. It was the 16th day of the month.

On his way home from the hospital that day, my father stopped by the office of the local weekly newspaper, The Mahomet Sucker State, and dropped off a birth announcement.

The notice was printed the day after my birth. Was it foreshadowing or a coincidence that my name appeared in print so quickly after I made my grand appearance?

Naomi Hillman and Jim Kroner, engagement picture.

Of course, I have no memory of this, but having seen the newspaper clipping, can confirm its accuracy.

Memories are interesting.

Do we really recall the details we profess to know or have we heard the stories so many times they are imbedded in our minds?

Before the age of 5, I really have only three memories of which I am positive. 1) We lived east of Mahomet at the site which eventually became the Tincup Camper's Park. 2) There was a cattle crossing at the end of the driveway, though I have no actual memory of our family having livestock.

The third memory is more vivid.

I woke up one evening at what must have been the darkest part of the night to the sounds of thrashing and pounding in my room from wall to wall and, occasionally, from wall to window.

I don't think I've screamed so loud since then.

My mother came to investigate and told me it was just a bat. Just a bat? I remember wondering if it wasn't a person swatting a baseball bat.

And that is the story behind how I slept with a nightlight on the remainder of the two years I lived on that property.

There is another memory, but only because I heard about it several times after Interstate 74 from Champaign to Mahomet opened in October, 1967. My mom and I would be driving home, and as we passed a certain point about a half-mile west of what is now Prairieview Road, she'd say, "We're now driving on what was once our farm land."

My parents had left that farmstead about seven years before the highway was built, so I don't know exactly how much acreage was taken away from the property. All I know is that the pasture land, where I had ridden on the fender of a tractor going about 3 mph was now a concrete pathway where our car was traveling 60-plus mph.

That old neighborhood was never the same. Houses and subdivisions soon started sprouting up to the east. We used to see nothing but farmland in that direction. Today, it's one home after another.

I take pride in calling Mahomet my home, though for reasons that have little to do with the amenities.

For the last 130 years – at least – someone from my immediate family has had a Mahomet address. I use that wording because more than half of those years, it was a rural Mahomet address and not 'in' the Village Limits.

Both sets of grandparents spent the majority of their lives in or around Mahomet or Mansfield.

Of my first 64 years, all but seven have been with a Mahomet address. Four of the exceptions were when I was a student at the University of Illinois, and living in Champaign. The other three were when my first job took me to McLean County, and a just-finished townhouse in Bloomington.

We lived on East St., even though there was a lot of Bloomington to the east of our location along the border of Illinois Wesleyan University. There were five townhouses in the complex. We lived in No. 3. At the time we moved in, the other two had not yet been rented.

Those units no longer exist. They were torn down after a lifespan of barely two decades to make room for a new Illinois Wesleyan University baseball diamond, Horenberger Field. I once sat in the bleachers there watching a game, sitting in a seat that – as best as I could recall – was where my living room would have been. That was surreal.

My life in Mahomet has been split almost 50-50 between living the country life and residing in town. In 2019, the in-town residency took the lead, 29 years to 28 years.

At this point, it looks like the Mahomet tradition will end with me as I am the lone remaining Kroner in the community. Rather than view that with sadness, I prefer to consider fondly the century-plus legacy our family will be leaving behind.

Fred's Favorites

FAVORITE SINGERS/GROUPS
1. Harry Chapin
2. Jim Croce
3. REO Speedwagon
4. Dan Seals
5. Creedence Clearwater Survival
6. Billy Joel

CHAPTER TWO

Age has a way of changing perspectives.

If this book had been written decades ago, the focus of my childhood would have been on how much I hated being an only child.

I felt it ruined my first 17 years.

As I have matured, it became clear that being an only child only contributed to the ruination of my first 17 years.

Equally bad was growing up in a rural area AND being an only child. The closest neighbor with children lived a mile away. That was my classmate, Randy Primmer. His family lived on the same road (2600 N), directly to the west. To the northwest were brothers Rick and Tim Roy. Rick was a year ahead of me in school. Tim was a couple of years behind me.

I learned to entertain myself and do things that didn't require a companion.

I read every book in the Chip Hilton series, written by former college basketball coach Clair Bee. I even wrote a book, some 150 hand-written pages, where the main character was named Speed Jones. I don't remember the name of his sidekick, but he had one just like Chip Hilton had his trustworthy buddy, Soapy Smith.

I was convinced my book would be a best-seller; maybe the first time an author would have that distinction before he was a teen-ager. I mailed it off to different publishing houses. Almost immediately, Random House responded, "no, thanks."

Grosset and Dunlap, and others, did, too.

Finally, I couldn't send it out any more. My only copy wasn't returned and I had forgotten where I had sent it last.

Reading, writing and playing table-top sports games consumed my young life when I wasn't doing farm work.

We moved to the only childhood home I remember, 5 miles north of Mahomet, in November, 1960 at a homestead my parents had designed. It was shortly after my fifth birthday. Moving Day was accompanied by snow flurries.

That year, and for the next several years, I had one item and only one item on my Christmas wish list. To anybody who would listen I asked for, "a little brother or a little sister. I don't care which."

My request went unfulfilled. Many of my friends, who had siblings, told me how lucky I was not to share clothes or a room or have an argument about which TV shows to watch.

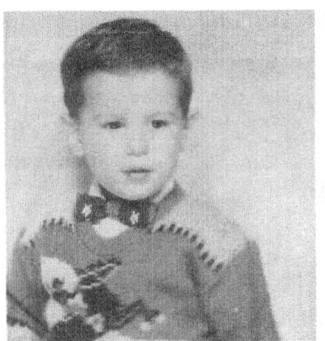

Christmas Card, circa 1959, age 4.

They said I was the fortunate one. I wish I could have traded places with any of them.

In my heart, I knew THEY were the ones who were blessed. THEY had what I wanted, what I craved, what I

THE FACES OF FRED KRONER

1961-62, First Grade.

1962-63, Second Grade.

1963-64, Third Grade.

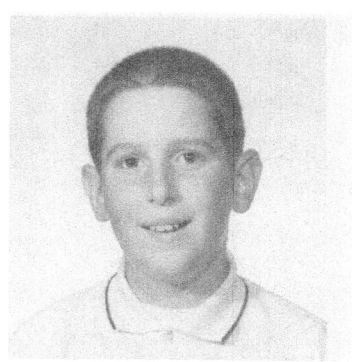

1965-66, Fifth Grade.

1969-70, Freshmen.

1972-73, Senior.

needed. They weren't lonely or forced to play by themselves hour-after-hour, day-after-day, month-after-month.

I had friends who lived in town and only had to cross the street to have a playground and basketball court available. Nearby for them was a baseball diamond and a grassy area for kickball or pickup football games.

All I was surrounded by was acres and acres of dirt and miles and miles of nothingness.

Fred's Favorites

FAVORITE SONGS
1. Piano Man (Billy Joel)
2. Lady (Styx)
3. Time in a Bottle (Jim Croce)
4. Brandy (Looking Glass)
5. One Friend (Dan Seals)]
6. Can't You See (Marshall Tucker Band)

CHAPTER THREE

Walter Alston was one of my first heroes and inspirations. He achieved his dream, perhaps not in the way he would have anticipated as a youngster; but he reached a level I am sure he must have dreamed about.

Alston spent 23 years in the major leagues. He is a Hall-of-Famer.

Checking his career biography, the statistical sheet shows that he played in one major league baseball game, batted one time and struck out.

He didn't give up. He turned his focus from playing to managing.

Alston was in charge of the Brooklyn and later Los Angeles Dodgers for 23 years. His teams won seven National League pennants and claimed four World Series championships. As a manager, his teams won more than 2,000 games.

Most of my childhood friends would probably say I was the biggest sports fan they knew. Especially when it came to baseball and basketball and, to a lesser extent, football. We talked sports daily and wrote out sports quizzes for each other.

This was a regular ritual for myself, Wally Pierce, Robert Herbst and, at times, Jeff Hinton. We had trivia questions, player names to unscramble, fill in the blank and true/false questions. We would find each other before the start of the school day, exchange our hand-written sports quizzes and then return them the following day with the anticipation of another one.

Keep in mind, this was before the creation of the internet or Google. We got our information from the backs of baseball cards, from the newspaper sports sections or magazines.

For some reason, I remember the hardest question I ever asked on one of these quizzes. It was fill-in-the-blank and it was from my senior year in 1973. "Name two current major league players who have the exact same letters in their last name, but who have different last names."

I finally had to give my friends the answer. It was Rick R-E-U-S-C-H-E-L and Ron S-C-H-U-E-L-E-R, both of whom were pitchers and early in their major league careers that spring.

My personal highlight, however, had occurred during the 1969 season. I memorized the starting lineup and batting order for every National League team. Each morning as I waited outside for the school bus, I recited all of the lineups so they would be etched in my mind.

To this day, I can still recall the regular lineup and batting order that season for the Leo Durocher-managed Chicago Cubs in their heartbreak season.

Don Kessinger, shortstop
Glenn Beckert, second base
Billy Williams, left field
Ron Santo, third base
Ernie Banks, first base
Randy Hundley, catcher
Jim Hickman, right field
Don Young, center field
Ferguson Jenkins, pitcher

The right field and center field positions were shared by different players. Oscar Gamble was in there at times. So were Al Spangler, Jimmy Qualls and Adolfo Phillips. Jenkins, of course, was only the pitcher every fifth game, but when I did the lineups it was always with the pitching aces.

I couldn't have imagined it at the time, but I eventually interviewed two of those players – Hundley and Williams – before I retired as a sportswriter.

My interest in sports was undeniable. My playing career was virtually non-existent.

I could accept it all these years later without bitterness if I were convinced in my mind that I wasn't good enough. I'll never know.

My father used the excuse that living in the country, miles from town, precluded me from participating in activities like the kids who lived in town and could walk home, or to practice, could do.

Little League baseball was open to youngsters ages 10, 11 and 12. I begged and pleaded – and yes, whined and cried – and was finally able to play as an 11- and 12-year-old.

Our family had one car, and no interest in getting a second one. My mother worked part-time as a bookkeeper on the UI campus. She worked at Randolph School Supply, on Sixth Street. The Quonset hut building is now gone. In its place is Joe's Brewery.

My father needed access to a car for the unexpected times an implement would break down and parts were needed.

We worked out a deal. My parents agreed to get me to every Little League game, but not to any practices. When there were Saturday practices – and those happened most weeks – I could ride my two-speed red Schwinn bicycle (which I still own!) to the practice field. Taking the rural roads that I needed to follow (in other words, avoiding traveling on Illinois Rt. 47), it was just shy of a 6-mile one-way trip.

It was worth every second.

I was selected to play for the Dodgers. There were three other teams in the Mahomet league, the Cubs, the Cardinals and the Braves. I was, of course, disappointed not to be on the Cubs, but elated to be on any team.

The Mahomet league had a rule that every game a kid was at, they were required to play a minimum of two innings. That was good. It meant the coaches couldn't hold it against me for not attending the weeknight practices.

I even had my career highlight as an 11-year-old, though I didn't know at the time it would be the lone high point. The Dodgers were playing the Cubs and we were facing perhaps the fastest pitcher in Mahomet at that time, Bill Cook. If he wasn't the fastest, he was certainly in the upper group, right beside left-hander Tom Bernett, who was taller and thus more intimidating.

Regardless of who was pitching, I always got my cuts. I took very few called strikes.

My turn to bat against Cook came in the third inning and I swung late on a fast ball. It was traveling down the right field line and, somehow, stayed fair and went over the fence. As I neared second base, one of my good friends, Robert Herbst, said, "I can't believe you hit a home run."

I couldn't either!

Every game, my mother had a decision to make. In order to be efficient, she would do her grocery shopping at the IGA during a part of the game. She would wait to see if I was in the starting lineup. If so, she stayed until the third inning. If not, she would leave immediately and try to be back by the third inning.

It wasn't a foolproof system for her because some days the checkout lanes were longer than other days or she had more items on her list to find.

On this particular late afternoon, she said she pulled into the parking lot to see me rounding third base and heading for home. She missed seeing the actual hit, but got to see the celebration at the plate.

I wasn't a kid who always looked for her prior to an at-bat, so I wasn't aware she had missed it until we were heading home that afternoon. I felt worse for her than for me. It didn't diminish the accomplishment.

As excited as I was about the opposite-field homer, I was even more excited to know that I would get recognition in the weekly newspaper. The Sucker State ran box scores of all Little League games and had a short writeup where they also mentioned the first names of those who hit home runs or had a lot of strikeouts.

At 11 years old, I learned how unfair newspapers can be. My memorable game occurred on a Wednesday, which meant it was past the deadline needed to get it published that week in the Thursday edition.

It turns out, the editors of The Sucker State, the Pugh family, took a one-week vacation annually in late July. The vacation was the week after my home run. I thought it meant I just had to wait an additional seven days to get my first newspaper clipping.

When the paper was delivered that was 15 days after my hit, it was like everything that occurred the week of my home run hadn't actually happened. There were Little League box scores all right, along with the roundups, but they skipped that week and went directly to the following week.

At least I have a good memory.

By the time I reached junior high, basketball was pretty much an equal passion for me as baseball. I found out when practices started my seventh-grade year and excitedly gave all the information to my parents.

None of my classmates had participated in any kind of

travel league or AAU program, so we were on equal footing, except that many of them had ample pickup games at one of the outdoor courts in town.

There was nothing I could do, however, to convince my parents to let me have a shot. They had more reasons than I had fingers. My transportation to and from school each day was the yellow school bus. The district didn't offer bus service after practices to get me home.

I absolutely couldn't have another parent bring me home because then we would be obligated to them and it's never a good thing to owe somebody something, they said. My mother didn't have a set work schedule and wouldn't always be available to pick me up. If the roads were snowy or icy, our car wouldn't leave the garage.

And so on.

It's the only time I can recall an argument with raised voices between my father and grandfather (his father). I remember vividly my grandpa saying, "Jim, you've got to let the boy have some fun."

One thing about my father was that he always steadfastly consistent. No one told him what to do. Not family. Not anyone. He was bound and determined to ruin – excuse me, to run – my life.

The answer to my request to play basketball as a seventh-, eighth- and ninth-grader was no, no and NO.

Had I been smart, I would have left it there, but I begged again as a high school sophomore. This time, to my shock and amazement, the answer was "yes." I never asked what changed his mind; I didn't care.

The approval came with the stipulation that I had to tell the coach I might miss some practices if I had no way to get home afterwards. I'm sure I told my parents I had that conversation.

I was optimistic about my prospects because in noon-hour

pickup basketball games, I was somebody several of the kids wanted on their teams.

Translation: As one of the taller kids, I could rebound and they didn't need to be concerned about me taking outside shots away from them, since that was out of my range.

What I neglected to take into account is that the noon-hour games are half-court, so speed and agility weren't as important as in the full-court version.

The first day of practice started out more exciting for me than any Christmas morning. Ever. Bill Harner was the coach. He had been one of my teachers in junior high, so he at least knew my name.

There's something that should be made clear now. There are certain expectations that are just a given. For example, if a sixth-grader is asked to write a three-paragraph essay, it is naturally assumed that he or she knows his ABCs and can write words.

As a high school sophomore on the basketball court, there are certain aspects that shouldn't need explaining. Coach Harner allowed us a few minutes for free shooting before he blew his whistle and had us hit the end line in three equal groups of five.

"We'll do the weave," he said.

At this point, I had never heard of a weave, participated in a weave or even seen a weave. As I stood clueless, Coach Harner told me to watch the first group and then fall into line.

I wasn't a quick learner. When my threesome went out, the passes for me went to where I was supposed to be, not where I actually was, and when I finally retrieved the ball, my pass went to the wrong teammate. Repeatedly.

Be careful what you wish for, I thought as I showered after practice. My dream seemed more like a nightmare.

I successfully made it through the first semester, though

my mastery of the weave never happened. I am perhaps the only person who can recall the details of every high school basketball game in which they played.

There were two.

My debut was at DeLand-Weldon in our second sophomore game. I made an appearance during the final two minutes and grabbed one defensive rebound. My finale was at Farmer City in our third game. I had one minute of court time and again grabbed a defensive rebound.

I never got to play in a game on my home court and my parents never attended any of the games, whether it was ones I played in or sat on the bench.

There were practices over Christmas Break, but my parents decided I wouldn't be at them. The team had a Christmas Tournament and when I showed up for the designated bus departure time, Coach Harner pulled me aside and said I was welcome to go to the game and to be in uniform, but he couldn't play me since I had missed a week's worth of practices.

It was the last time I wore uniform No. 40.

The following day, I talked to the coach about what I could do to remain a part of the team. He agreed to take me on as a second manager with the understanding I only had to go to the games and, if I didn't miss any, I would earn my numerals.

He was true to his word.

I think it's worth noting that our sophomore team basketball won-lost record that year was 10-12, but in the games I played, we were 2-0.

The other main basketball manager, incidentally, was my neighbor, Rick Roy.

I never tried out for another sports team at Mahomet-Seymour. Fate worked against me.

Baseball wasn't offered at the high school level until the

spring of my junior year, 1972. By then, I was coming straight home from school each day that it wasn't raining and helping prepare the fields to be planted.

Since junior high, when my father decided he was physically unable to withstand the rigors of being on a tractor for extended periods of time, the arrangement we had was that he did all of the maintenance work and I did all of the field work, except for the planting and harvesting. My uncle, Don Turner, handled that since we didn't own a planter or a combine.

To this day, I am convinced I could have played some high school baseball, but I am thankful for Walter Alston being the role model that showed me that if you can't reach your main dream, you can reach a revised dream and it's still pretty darned good.

I was busy transferring my passion for sports from the competitive element to that of being a writer. The very same Mahomet Sucker State – the newspaper which overlooked my one and only home run – was now running my byline each week for M-S sports roundups.

What more could a teen-ager want?

CHAPTER FOUR

To understand my start in newspaper writing, it's
necessary to know the school lunch policy during my
junior high years.

Lunch was 30 cents a day, or $1.50 per week. An extra milk
was either four or five cents apiece.

My mother would give me lunch money for the week on
Monday mornings. During the winter months, it usually
went to lunch.

During the spring and fall, I found other plans for this
bounty. There was no sign-in sheet or sign-out sheet for lunch
at the junior high school and the school doors were never
locked once they were opened for the day.

During baseball season, there was always an ample supply
of baseball cards at one of the stores uptown. I usually went
to Chuck's Drug Store, but I might wind up across the street
at Eisner's, too.

A pack of cards was five cents and I don't remember paying
tax. Surely, I did. Each pack consisted of five cards and a
stick of bubble gum.

I had no interest whatsoever in the bubblegum. Various
friends loved the gum – though I can't imagine why – and I

would either trade with them for more cards or an apple or something from their sack lunches. I almost always wound up with something to eat for lunch, but I was always more than ready for supper!

My mother chalked my hunger up to being a growing boy.

Even though the junior high school was only three or four blocks from the downtown area, for some reason my friends and I took a path that was behind the houses located on the north side of Main Street, instead of following the sidewalks. We got yelled at more than once by the property owners, but that didn't deter us.

It didn't get us there any quicker, and if we thought we were being secretive and not being seen, it didn't matter much as soon as we entered the stores. There always seemed to be someone who recognized our faces. That tends to happen in communities with about 1,300 residents, as the population sign for Mahomet read in the early 1970s.

All of this is to explain that during August, September and October, as well as in February, March, April and May, I was a regular noontime visitor downtown.

I was already an avid reader and scoured through every page of the daily and weekly newspapers which were delivered to our home.

I took note of what was included. And, what was not included.

The weekly Mahomet Sucker State never seemed to have any coverage of the local junior high sports teams. One February day, hauling a bag of baseball card packets I had just purchased, I opened the door of the Mahomet Sucker State, then located on Dunbar Street.

An elderly gentleman got up from the typesetting machine to see what I wanted. I explained that I always found coverage of the local high school sports teams each week, but never read anything about the junior high teams.

The man, Joe Pugh, told me that the paper had only a few employees and they were responsible for writing the stories, writing the headlines, laying out the pages, selling advertisements, setting the type, getting the papers to the post office and there was just not time to add coverage of the junior high.

As I turned to leave, he added, "If someone were to give us the articles, we would publish them."

I considered that an invitation to write. Starting the following week, in February of 1968, I had a short three- or four-paragraph byline story in the community newspaper. I continued submitting stories – never receiving as much as a free newspaper – until I graduated from high school in 1973.

As I moved from junior high to the high school, my coverage area shifted to the older levels, thus ending the brief coverage devoted to the seventh- and eighth-grade teams.

I didn't have access to a typewriter at home, so all stories during those years were handwritten and turned in on pieces of legal-sized yellow paper. Every Monday, rain or snow or sunlight, I made the trek to the newspaper office, even on those winter days when there were no baseball cards for sale.

I took the sidewalk, too.

It doesn't take a rocket scientist to figure that a young person writing sports stories with no experience or training doesn't provide compelling content. The phrase, "it was better than nothing," comes to mind, but in truth I think a note is necessary: Barely.

Virtually every story began with me first identifying the day and date. One week's story would start, "On Friday, Dec. 3…" The next week's article began, "On Friday, Dec. 10…"

In high school, I made the faux pas of mixing commentary with the facts.

The M-S varsity boys' basketball coach, Merv Correll, called me into his office one day. It wasn't to offer a compliment.

He immediately made reference to my most recent story, which started, "Against two teams that should have been pushovers, the Bulldogs split two contests last week."

Correll lectured me about how the score is always 0-0 at the start of the game and that sometimes teams have injured players, which affects the quality of play, or an injured player just returned to the lineup to bolster a team, or sometimes a particular player would get a hot hand and be unstoppable or the team's top player would endure a bad game, but it all resulted in there being no pushovers in the sporting world, at any level.

I listened politely and didn't argue, but later laughed with my buddies about the conversation. I had seen the games and was convinced my basic premise was correct: Those teams should have been pushovers.

However, there was a point the coach didn't specifically make, but which I learned about years later in journalism school. Factual stories are one kind of articles and commentaries are a totally different and separate kind. Opinions should never be inserted into a factual story.

So, in fact, I was wrong to have written the story the way I did by interjecting my opinion. I'm pretty sure that during the next 50-plus years of sportswriting, I never referred to a team as a pushover.

Something else happened in junior high, which years later had a profound effect on my life.

In Language Arts, we had to do a Career Day project. Each of us were asked to research a profession that we might have an interest in. We were required to have at least one source from a person with that job, to prevent us from simply regurgitating what was found in an encyclopedia.

Anyone want to guess what profession I picked?

Champaign-Urbana was still the home of two daily

newspapers in 1968, The News-Gazette and The Morning Courier.

I wrote to the sports editor of each publication. Loren Tate was at The News-Gazette and Lon Eubanks was at The Courier. Eubanks responded within days. I never heard from Tate.

This story didn't end when the grades were issued for the assignment, however.

The conclusion would take place six full years later, in August of 1974. I was visiting at my parents' house shortly before my sophomore year at the University of Illinois was to start, when the phone rang.

I answered it and heard a voice say, "I am calling for Fred Kroner."

"You have him," I said.

"This is Lon Eubanks," the voice said as my eyes and ears perked up.

"You had contacted me some years ago about an interest in sportswriting. I don't know what you're doing now, but if you are still interested, we have an opening for a scoretaker and could put you to work three nights a week."

I didn't need time to think. "When can I start," I immediately asked.

He laughed and said things would get going the week after Labor Day.

It was an entry-level position and involved no in-person coverage, just taking a plethora of results by telephone and writing a three-paragraph summation. I was one of three scoretakers that school year, joining a part-time team that also included Rob Fink and Karen Richards.

I was so blown away by the opportunity that the obvious questions didn't come to mind. How had he gotten my phone number? When I wrote to him in junior high, we didn't have a home phone. Had he really saved my letter all those years?

I had never followed up or applied for a job there, thinking experience was necessary in order to be hired.

That's one mystery that likely won't be solved.

Fred's Favorites

FAVORITE COACHES TO INTERVIEW
1. Mike Hebert (UI volleyball)
2. Scott Thomas (Sullivan girls' basketball)
3. Chris Mennig (St. Thomas More, Urbana girls' basketball)
4. Lee Cabutti (Champaign Central boys' basketball)
5. Terri Sullivan (UI softball)
6. Karrie Redeker (Unity, Parkland women's basketball)

CHAPTER FIVE

I almost didn't enroll at the University of Illinois.

I applied there and at Illinois State University in Normal, and was accepted by both institutions.

It truly didn't matter to me which one I attended.

My father had plenty of ideas. He made it clear the UI was my best choice. I could live at home, save money and be available to help on the farm.

To me, that was three strikes against the idea.

That wasn't the trifecta I was seeking. The more he pushed, the more appealing I found ISU, only because I knew I would be living on campus.

As a UI graduate, my father considered it important that I carry on the family tradition. He finally asked what it would take for me to pick the UI.

I said my decision would be based on whether I could live on campus and if that was an option at Illinois, I could see myself going there.

That ended the discussion about colleges, but not my wait.

Like most colleges, the UI held a New Student Week which began on a Sunday with classes scheduled to start not the next day, but on Monday of the following week.

New Student Week arrived and I was packed and ready to go. My father kept finding work that had to be finished up on the farm. Sunday passed. Then Monday. And Tuesday.

Wednesday came and left. Same for Thursday and Friday. Saturday was more of the same.

Finally, on Sunday afternoon – 18 hours before my first class – my mom took me to Room 440 Hopkins Hall.

Most of my final week at home had been devoted to planning ways to never again spend a night in that single-story country brick house.

I almost succeeded.

I returned for five days during Thanksgiving Break of my freshman year and the first two nights of Christmas Break the following month.

After that, I'd made arrangements to house sit for a group of guys who lived at the northeast corner of Springfield and Wright streets, in Urbana. They even paid me $150 cash to stay there by myself and watch their TV for three weeks.

That was maybe the best "job" I ever had.

During Spring Break of my freshman year, I joined a small group of students – none of whom I knew – on a trip to Fort Lauderdale, Fla. I left campus with $50 and returned a week later with two one-dollar bills.

For the summer of 1974, I committed to a sales job with the Southwestern Company. They put us up for a week in the Master Host Inn, in Nashville, for training before sending us to various destinations. Mine was Hagerstown, Md.

Three of us were sent to that area to sell Bibles – and related items – door to door. Because of our mission, a local church agreed to put us up on cots in their basement.

The summer taught me a valuable lesson, whatever I did in life had better not involve sales. I sold one Bible in 10 weeks.

It was supposed to be a 12-week commitment, but the way the UI was scheduled, I had to leave after 10 weeks. Good thing, too, because the one afternoon I stopped by to visit my parents when I returned was the day the call from Lon Eubanks came.

And that year, I was able to experience the full scope of New Student Week, again at Room 440 Hopkins Hall.

My roommates from the previous year, Gregg Jarman and Peter Gray, were a year older and had arranged off-campus accommodations. My sophomore year roommates were two of my fellow graduates from the M-S Class of 1973, Robert Herbst and Steve Traub.

I had started working for Food Service at my dorm and was able to stay on campus during the Thanksgiving and Christmas breaks that year as the university kept one dorm open for foreign students who weren't able to get home. They needed to be fed, so by agreeing to work, I got my meals, too, that otherwise wouldn't have been part of my room and board package.

I had a second Florida trip for Spring Break of my sophomore year, and moved into my first apartment, on Bradley Ave., just north of Kraft, the day after that semester ended.

What I was learning wasn't necessarily the subjects being taught in the UI classrooms.

By working Food Service both semesters of my sophomore year, combined with the scoretaker duties at The Courier (which was more like four nights most weeks; not three), there was less and less time to study. My status as a Dean's List student from my first college semester was gone.

I wasn't in danger of being put on probation, but the College of Communications decided they had more qualified candidates for what would have been the start of my junior year in August, 1975.

I had completed all of my two years of liberal arts classes and needed to declare a major and pursue those requirements. I had no backup plan, so decided to take the 1975-76 school year off and focus on work at The Courier.

I also joined the overnight staff at f IGA (on Glen Park Drive) in west Champaign. My shift was supposed to start at 11 p.m. and end at 7 a.m. On nights I worked at The Courier, I seldom left the newsroom before 11:30. By the time I'd drive from Race Street, in Urbana, to the IGA, I was usually clocking in about midnight.

I enjoyed the night crew. Jerry Metcalf Jr. was a gem and I got to work with one of the delightful Centennial High School athletes I had gotten to know through covering the Chargers' baseball team, Billy May.

My path continued to cross with Billy May. He spent time as a high school basketball coach at Potomac and later – after moving to Mahomet – had children whom I covered in sports.

Even though I was saving the IGA management an hour of pay most nights of the week, as the summer of '76 approached, Ayr-Way decided they didn't need my help any more.

Their decision came at an opportune time. I had re-enrolled at the UI, but hadn't paid the fees for the 1976-77 school year. With the help of my colleagues at The Courier, I had a good recommendation to take with me to the College of Communications admissions officers and this time, they welcomed me. Ironic, isn't it, that they accepted me a year after they denied me admission and I'd done nothing in the year off to improve my grade-point average?

There was plenty of change in my life in the final months of 1976, leaving the grocery store, returning to school. And, I'd just gotten married.

Fred's Favorites

FAVORITE MOVIES
1. The Natural
2. The Jazz Singer
3. Evita
4. The Post
5. Green Mile
6. Out of Africa

CHAPTER SIX

I haven't yet mentioned the one portion of my childhood which probably had the greatest real-life impact.

My parents enrolled me in school a year sooner than should have been allowed. I started kindergarten as a four-year-old and was five most of the first semester of my first-grade year.

With a November birthday, I was supposed to have been held back, but it didn't work out that way. I was never told the reason. Many years later, I learned some of my classmates also had November birthdays – but were born a full year before me.

The difference was most evident once I was in high school. I turned 16 in November of my junior year.

Many of my classmates, with birthdays earlier in the year, celebrated No. 16 months sooner and thus were in driver's education class by the end of their sophomore years.

I didn't get to the behind-the-wheel phase until the spring semester of my junior year. It was the end of May of my junior year before I got my actual license.

Until then … No license. No access to a car. No dating. No fun.

Getting my license right before the start of summer might

sound like a good thing, but not so much for someone facing hours upon hours of summer work on the farm.

Back then, we not only tilled the soil in preparation for planting, but we also usually ran over the ground with a rotary hoe after the seeds were in the ground to help them emerge. We then cultivated the land to get rid of weeds in between the rows and, for corn fields, there was often another trip between the rows with the tractor trailed by a sprayer.

Always on the to-do list was walking the hundreds of rows of soybeans (planted in quarter-mile rows) to pull or cut out the milkweeds, cockleburs and butterprint as well as volunteer corn. I don't remember a year where I got completely through with every bean field by the time the harvest started.

As much as I detested the task of walking the beans as a solo worker, it was on those summer days that my passion for baseball was sparked.

I was never paid for any of the farm work I did, nor did I have an allowance. My father said I could consider my pay to be the clothes they bought or the food I ate or the fees they paid (such as the physical exam I needed to try out for basketball as a sophomore).

However, my mother recognized my need for money now and then, so as she collected S&H Green Stamps, she gave them to me as well as the books needed to put them in. She had a catalog that showed items which customers could get in exchange for a certain number of books of Green Stamps. The bigger the item, the larger the number of Green Stamp books that were required.

There was a redemption center on Prospect Avenue, in Champaign, just north of where Judah Christian is now located, and a block before the intersection with Bradley Ave.

Even before I played Little League baseball, I had filled enough books for her to get an item. I requested a transistor radio. I looped it around my belt when I was walking beans. For a time, listening to music on Chicago's WLS was satisfying, but when you're in the fields for 9 or 10 hours a day, some tunes were played three or four times and that became boring very soon.

I started turning the dial and discovered baseball games on WGN. Because the Chicago Cubs played all of their home games during the day in the 1960s and 1970s (as well as most of the 1980s), I literally grew up listening to broadcasters Vince Lloyd and Lou Boudreau. Many days, I stayed in the bean fields longer to be able to hear the end of a ball game.

The biggest issue was having enough batteries to keep the transistor operational. My mother routinely added them to the weekly grocery list. She knew how important it was for me to have that outlet.

For years, I took the radio to bed with me when the Cubs were on a West Coast tour. I credit that with my ability to stay awake and alert until midnight or 1 a.m., a trait which is still with me. As long as there were batteries in the house, I seldom missed the end of a Cubs' game.

By the time I got into driver's ed classes at the high school, I had been driving tractors for seven years. It's not the same, of course. I don't think the old (1945) Allis Chalmers WD went more than 3 or 4 mph, but it provided me plenty of tries to learn to use a stick shift and not slip the clutch.

That experience didn't count with the driver's ed teacher – Mr. Correll, the basketball coach – but it gave me plenty of confidence as I moved up to vehicles that could easily travel 60 or 70 mph.

I enjoyed having the license in my wallet, but it didn't help me get to school as a senior. We still had just the one car, a blue and white 1960 Chevrolet Belair, and riding the school bus was a requirement for the 12th year in a row so that my parents always had the car available, if needed.

Most disappointing was the spring day some of the other farm kids organized a Drive Your Tractor to School day. I had to take the bus that day, too, but enjoyed seeing all of the John Deere and International Harvester tractors in the school parking lot over the lunch break.

With limited chances to use the car, I didn't date much. I went to Prom as a senior, but returned home before the Post Prom event started at Western Bowl, in Champaign.

I thought college would offer a breakthrough, but what I learned about myself was that I didn't enjoy the getting-to-know-someone-well-enough-to ask-them-out part. My focus was elsewhere even if my mind wasn't.

Fred's Favorites

FAVORITE ACTORS
1. Michael Douglas
2. Robert DeNiro
3. Robin Williams
4. Jack Nicholson
5. Denzel Washington
6. Tom Hanks

CHAPTER SEVEN

I've been blessed to have had a number of influential women in my life, including my mother, who is the subject of another section.

I remember my first crush. She was the epitome of beauty and elegance, grace and Hollywood glamour.

She was the daughter of my mom's boss. Her given name was Virginia, but she preferred to be called Ginny.

She was 11 years older than me, but always had a few minutes for the youngster sitting in the corner playing with army men that were generally stored in her father's cigar box, when she would stop by the office.

My mom worked part-time, once a week at the most and often just once every two weeks. The only guarantee was that she would be in the office on payday, or the previous day, to write the payroll checks.

From the time I was 6 or 7, I was allowed to accompany her in the summer because the vast majority of business for the Randolph School Supply Company was mail order. It was rare for anyone other than a salesman or one of the Randolph children – Patricia, Bobby, Billy or Ginny – to walk through the doors.

There were maybe five or six times a year I was fortunate enough to see Ginny. She was always ooohing and aaahing at the marks on the wall where her father measured my height the first day I returned each year. He would write the year beside the black line he drew.

It made me feel important that he wanted to do that. And, it was really special that Ginny noticed and made a big deal about it. She was so sweet to give me the attention.

It always made me wish I had siblings.

Several years after my mother passed, I received the nicest letter from Ginny. She was living in Georgia at the time with her family. She told me how much the whole family thought of my mother and she sent me her notary seal.

It's a special keepsake I've cherished, along with her hand-written letter. Some gifts really are priceless.

Ginny passed away too soon (2003), interestingly at the same age my mother was when she died in 1985.

*

My first girlfriend was one I found through my first job, at the Champaign-Urbana Morning Courier.

Phyllis wasn't a co-worker, but a correspondent who regularly reported sports results from Octavia High School, in Colfax.

As the newbie at The Courier, I learned to appreciate those who knew what they were doing when they phoned. It wasn't a good combination when the newly hired scoretaker was matched with someone so unfamiliar with the process they would ask, "What information do you need?"

That's why the expression, "the blind leading the blind," was created.

More often than not, I wound up missing some important detail like the time the home team won its football game, 21-20, after scoring the only touchdown of the fourth quarter. I neglected to ask at what point that TD was scored.

Sure enough, The News-Gazette (the competition!) highlighted the player scoring the winning TD in the final minute.

Phyllis and her cohorts at Octavia were as sharp as newly purchased knives. They were prepared and had all the needed information. The bad part was that usually made the calls go quickly.

She had the sweetest voice. Probably still does.

I think there were three girls who made calls from Octavia. They had two Champaign newspapers, another one in Bloomington and at least three television stations to contact, and they split up the duties.

The first time we talked was purely by chance. I happened to be the one who answered the phone and found myself talking to someone who was organized, efficient and had a very nice voice. It was my favorite call of the night.

The next Friday, when I arrived at my second-floor desk on Race Street, I asked my colleagues to put the call from Octavia on hold if I was on another line. I'm pretty sure after that week, she asked for me, too.

Or, maybe I just hoped she did.

By the time basketball season arrived, I was able to get out of the office and attend games on occasion. I volunteered to cover one that was scheduled at Octavia.

I let Phyllis know and she met me at the ticket booth. She had the unfair advantage of seeing me as I walked up the long sidewalk without me having a clue which one of the young ladies at the entrance might be her.

As I showed my ID, Mr. Jack Stimpert – the adult ticket-taker – told me that there was a person waiting to see me and she stepped out of the booth. I don't remember much about the game – in fact, I remember nothing about the game, like even who the Rockets were playing – but there was a mutual attraction that made the trip worthwhile.

It began a year of dating with my first serious girlfriend, and it continued through her first semester at Parkland College. One of us – me – was anxious to get married and the other – her – was not and that led to a split early in 1976.

But I soon got what I thought I wanted.

I was in my first apartment with two roommates I knew well from high school, Rick Durst and Bill Tigrak. We weren't exactly The Three Amigos. I was friends with both of them and they – usually – only tolerated each other.

Rick wasn't working and spent a lot of time at the apartment. When I got home one night, he told me there was a single girl living in the apartment above us and he was pretty sure she didn't have a boyfriend.

Her name was Donna.

Rick Durst, 1993.

He wanted me to go upstairs with him as he asked to borrow a cup of sugar. I swear that is the truth, as hokey as it seems.

We decided to wait for the weekend, which was another

two or three days away.

In the meantime, we started noticing extra activity in the stairway. Donna was getting a roommate. Rick and I took turns looking out the peephole while Bill chastised us for being juvenile. Instead, he threw knives at his bedroom door, which eventually prevented me from getting my damage deposit returned.

It made me wonder about the definition of juvenile!

Rick came up with a different plan. We would invite them to have a home-cooked meal with us, but since neither of us cooked anything more than pop tarts and pizza rolls, we would tell them that we would buy whatever food they wanted as long as they were willing to cook.

You think that worked?

I'm glad we didn't place a bet on it because I didn't think there was one chance in 100 they would say yes.

They said yes.

This was late February, 1976, at least a week after Valentine's Day.

That was when I was introduced to Dee Siddens.

In August of that year, we were married.

I had two years of college remaining. She had three years left.

Somehow, we thought this was a good idea.

What is it they say about hindsight?

Two years later, we added a housemate. We moved into a two-bedroom condo in Bloomington – on the west edge of the Illinois Wesleyan University campus – after I accepted my first full-time job, at the Bloomington Daily Pantagraph.

My cousin Tena Sprau was starting her first year at Illinois State University, which was less than a mile away to the north. It was much cheaper for her to live with us than in student housing.

I can't speak for the others, but it was an enjoyable two

years for me. Tena was one of the cousins who was closest to me in age, and we got along fantastically well together. I always considered her the sister I never had, so it was fitting that we shared the same residence.

A few years later (1983), I became exactly what I despised about my own childhood. I was the parent of an only child.

Our son, Devin, was born and was a true blessing. There is nothing I've found more awesome or memorable than seeing my child enter this world and take his first breath. OK, maybe I missed the first breath, but I got to see most of the ones that came in the first minute.

Raising a child is more than a full-time job, if you try to do it well. So is working as a sportswriter, if you try to do it well.

See the conflict developing?

I was accused of having a mistress and – in one sense – it was true. I was in love with my job. I was devoted to my job. I spent an incredible amount of time at my job, often leaving about 4 a.m. when the morning crew was starting to make its way into the building.

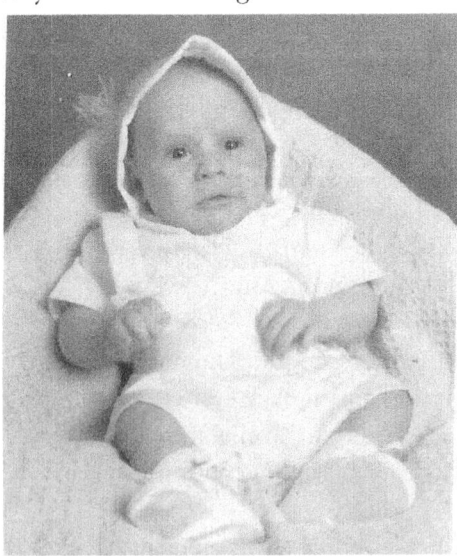

Devin Kroner,
April, 1983,
1-month old

I was fortunate to have a wife who was devoted to raising our son. More than once, probably more than 100 times, she told me what I was missing. "You spend more time watching other people's kids than you do your own," she said.

I never admitted it, of course, but she was right. I was on a merry-go-round that was spinning out of control and going faster and wilder as the years passed. It's impossible to step off without the whole ride – and your whole world – crashing around you.

While I loved the job, I didn't much like what it did to me or to the relationship I had with my wife. After 19 years together, we separated and divorced in 1995.

Thinking I should learn from past mistakes, I tried to cut back on work commitments and soon started a new relationship. Thanks to the Internet, chat rooms and instant messaging, I met Crystal Cool, who was living in Wyoming.

There was a part of me – a part that still exists – that believes in helping others and trying to be a part of the solution. Crystal was in a situation where she was living with her ex-husband in a trailer because she had nowhere else to go.

She wanted to finish school, but didn't have the money and had a disability that limited her ability to work and earn more than the essentials to exist from day to day.

We got married in 1996, she moved to Mahomet, enrolled at Parkland and earned her associate's degree in 1998. I was more in love with the idea of her having a better life than with her as a person. We divorced later in 1998, she returned to Wyoming, eventually moved to Texas and passed away in 2011.

I only know that from googling her name, because we never spoke again after she left.

*

Rather than shy away from another relationship, thinking

twice burned was enough, I jumped in again with both feet.

This time, it was with someone I had known for decades. Emily Moon and I were classmates at M-S from kindergarten through our graduation. Out of our graduating class of 99, about one-fourth of us were there together all 13 years.

There is a story that circulated about a fashion show we participated in as kids, probably first or second grade. It was sponsored by the Mahomet Town & Country Women's Club.

I have a vague recollection of the afternoon. I remember it was my time to go on stage and I was holding back. The girl behind me said, "C'mon. Let's go," and took my hand and led me out.

I've heard there is a newspaper clipping that will serve as verification, but it's not one I have seen.

According to several sources, the participants were lined up alphabetically, so it stands to reason that next to someone whose last named started with 'K' could be a person whose last name started with 'M.'

That person was Emily Moon, who was bold and outspoken, even as a child.

Years later, I actually asked Emily out when we were in college. I was at Illinois. She was at Iowa State. My roommate, Gregg Jarman, was a Star Course usher for many concerts at the Assembly Hall and he helped me get two good tickets for an upcoming Doobie Brothers concert.

I got Emily's address from her mother and wrote her a letter with all of the details. She responded quickly, but said since it was a mid-week concert, she couldn't make it over from Iowa as she had tests coming up.

Probably a legit reason, but she didn't leave the door partially open by saying she'd love to take a rain check, so I waited more than 25 years to ask her out again, after we reconnected at our class reunion in 1998 when she came up from Florida.

We were married in 1999 and blended her three children with my one, though none of us actually all lived under the same roof at the same time.

We can now tell people we have been married for more than 80 years because that's the total if you add my years of marriage to her cumulative total. They just haven't all been with each other.

If I want to sound really old, I tell people I have been married to Emily for two centuries, but I've learned that's usually the wrong thing to say.

While raising Devin, I was used to having just one child around at a time.

As I come face-to-face with retirement, there are plenty of young faces to keep me on my toes.

In all, there are seven grandchildren. Four belong to Devin and his wife, Elizabeth: Titus, Matthan, Larkin and Esli.

The other three are with Emily's middle son, Jamel Belahi, and his companion, Amber Anthony: Brayden Anthony, Addison Anthony and Preston Belahi.

Emily and Fred Kroner, June, 2015.

CHAPTER EIGHT

I was named after both of my grandfathers.

My paternal grandfather was Fred Kroner.

My maternal grandfather was Lewis Hillman.

My given name is Frederick Lewis Kroner.

It gets better.

When my paternal grandfather's given name is spoken, it sounds the same as mine: Frederick Louis Kroner.

The only way it could get even better is if my maternal grandfather was Lewis Frederick Hillman.

He wasn't, but his father – my great grandfather on my mom's side – was named John Fred Hillman.

I've reached the conclusion that virtually all of my relatives were (or are!) equally nice. I've felt closer to some, which I attribute to the opportunity to interact with them more.

From the time we moved to our new home north of Mahomet, in Newcomb Township, in 1960, there were very few Thursday and Saturday afternoons that Grandpa Kroner didn't stop by during the spring, summer and fall. Those were the afternoons he took off from his dental practice, which was housed in the Lewis Building, in downtown Champaign.

For a time, he also saw patients one day a week in Mahomet.

Because of his profession, my other cousins and I always referred to him as Grandpa Doc.

His usual pattern was to stop and visit with his four Turner grandchildren first – their house would be the first one he'd come to as he headed north out of town – and then stop by our residence.

I especially looked forward to his visits, especially after the spring rains had passed and we could be outside working in the garden. He would get right down in the dirt with me, teaching me how far apart to plant the various seeds, why we needed to make "hills" for the cucumbers and muskmelons, and the importance of weeding on a regular basis. And, much more.

We worked and we talked. He would share stories he knew about the sporting legends of the past, athletes who were no longer playing, but were ones I knew about because I was fascinated by sports history. He had seen Bob Feller – the man known as Rapid Robert – pitch and he knew all about the heroics of Lou Boudreau when he was a rare player-manager, primarily with the Cleveland Indians, in the major leagues.

We talked about so much more. He encouraged me to do well in school. "You'll need good grades to get into college and you need to get into college to get a good job," he said.

He told me about growing up in Mahomet, but yearning for more. After his junior year, he left the Mahomet school system and transferred to Champaign High for his senior year. He had an opportunity to be on the debate team there.

He didn't go directly into dental school after graduating with the Class of 1913. Instead, he explained how life was different in the early decades of the 1900s. Teachers didn't necessarily all have college degrees. He taught in Fisher for a year or two before heading to college.

More importantly, he allowed me opportunities my father would never consent to.

I'm guessing most people can't remember how many family vacations they went on during their childhood, how many sit-down restaurants they were at and how many sleepovers they were a part of.

I recall every one.

Zero, one and zero.

It was due to my grandfather's diligence that I went to a meal at the Hickory Hill Hunt Club, in rural White Heath. He and my grandmother, Edna Kroner– she was known as Nana to my cousins and myself – took me for no reason other than that I had never been to a restaurant.

I believe I was 9 or 10.

We were seated at a long table in the middle of the room with more silverware than I had ever seen at one place setting. Soon the salad arrived.

I dug in and within seconds heard my grandmother gasp, which led immediately to the most embarrassing moment of my life at that time.

Her words have stayed with me. "Haven't your parents taught you the difference in forks? Why aren't you using your salad fork?"

I couldn't speak. I was trying to choke back the tears, fearing I was being reprimanded for doing something wrong that I had no idea was wrong.

My grandfather came to my rescue, telling his wife that it was OK, sometimes people just use the first fork they pick up. He told me to continue eating and quietly added, "Usually the smaller fork is the one used for salads, but you wouldn't know that if you hadn't been told."

I didn't have to hear that message again, even though it was more than a decade later – when I was in college – that I was at another sit-down restaurant.

Another time, I remember coming into our house after school on a Thursday and my grandfather was already there. That was unusual. He hardly ever got to our house before the school bus arrived.

The room got quiet and finally my grandfather said to my father, "You should think about what I said."

I knew better than to ask then what they had been discussing, but I brought it up at supper that night. My father told me that Grandpa wanted to take me to a movie, but that he thought that was something to be saved for when I was older. I think I was 11.

A couple weeks later, Grandpa Doc drove me to Hoopeston to see the only movie I would see in a theater before graduating from high school. I was so in awe of the experience that I don't remember much about the movie except the title, "Gone With The Wind."

I've seen it numerous times on television since then and it conjures up a fond memory each time.

My grandpa had a fondness for spending his winters in Florida, along the Gulf Coast. As he aged into his 60s, he was cutting back on the number of patients he'd see and got away shortly after Christmas. He would stay through the baseball Spring Training season, in late March.

I would always benefit from his travels. He'd bring me back scorecards and programs from the games he saw, usually the Chicago White Sox, since he stayed close to where they trained in Sarasota.

I remember one year upon his return he told our family about how difficult it was to find a place to stay for his entire time away and he didn't like switching motels every few weeks, so he had solved the problem by buying one.

He was the proud owner of the Island House Motel, in

Nokomis, Fla. It remains in the family to this day.

It was through my grandfather's prodding that I entered produce in the Fisher Fair in the summer of 1970, after my freshman year. I'd never even been to a fair and was unaware

Island House, Nokomis, Fla.

that there was such a competition.

I submitted two entries. One received the blue ribbon. The other was given the red ribbon.

It gave me such a feeling of satisfaction and accomplishment. I had grown the produce, tended to it, picked it and then displayed it.

On Father's Day in 1971, my aunt and uncle — Carol and Don Turner – came over together late in the day. This was so unusual I knew it meant something special.

I can't remember a worse day in my life.

They had invited my grandfather out for lunch that day, but he didn't make it. When he didn't answer the phone, they drove to his home and found he had died in his sleep. My grandmother was the one with serious health issues and was blissfully unaware of what had taken place.

People find this hard to believe because my sportswriting career ultimately resulted in some major awards and recognitions coming my way, but the personal highlight for me had nothing to do with anything I ever accomplished.

It was the days I would be out and about somewhere, people would see my name and ask if I were related to the Fred Kroner who was the dentist.

Nothing makes me prouder than to say "yes, he was my grandfather."

When I started at The News-Gazette in 1981, this exchange would routinely happen two or three times a month. Gradually, it was reduced to two or three times a year. As late as 2015 – when I officially retired from The Gazette – I still got the question.

By then, it was 44 years since my grandfather had passed away and he was still remembered. That tribute means more to me than anything else that has ever happened – or will happen – in my life.

Fred's Favorites

FAVORITE ACTRESSES
1. Meryl Streep
2. Julia Roberts
3. Viola Davis
4. Hillary Swank
5. Jane Seymour
6. Halle Berry

Dr. Fred L. Kroner

CHAPTER NINE

Life is complicated and unpredictable. That has certainly been reflected in my life.

It's amazing that I spent so many years in the communications business. I was raised in a family that didn't communicate.

Throughout my teen-age years, I thought our family was the poorest of the poor. Those words were never spoken, but what else was I to think:

- We never went on a family vacation (not once);
- We didn't purchase as much as a window air-conditioner until I was a high school freshman and then only because my pediatrician at Christie Clinic said it would be helpful for me to cope with the severe hay fever I dealt with every fall;
- We didn't have a telephone until I was a high school sophomore;
- We didn't buy new clothes unless there was a specific need such as holes in the soles of my shoes or pants that barely went past my knees;
- We had a black and white television set, and when it broke, it wasn't replaced. Ever;
- We didn't eat at sit-down restaurants, but might get the Mr.

Quick special once a summer, five hamburgers for $1;

- When the family car was replaced in 1965, the "new" vehicle was a 1960 Chevrolet Belair, which was still our only car when I graduated from high school in 1973;

- When I was preparing for college, my mother took me to the old Commercial Bank (at the corner of University and First streets, where the Champaign Police Station is now located) and opened a checking account. A deposit was made for $150. The next time money was added, it was from my own earnings.

Occasionally there was an attempt at communication. It usually went like this:

Me: "May I …?"

My father: "No!"

For years, I had asked to have a party for my birthday. The idea was always rejected.

In fourth grade, on the spur of the moment, I decided I needed a party. On the bus ride home, two of the other passengers were my classmates, Vicki Henderson and Charlie O'Neal.

It was a Friday in mid-November. The next day was my birthday. I told them there would be a party at my house the next day and asked if they could come. They each thought they could.

I didn't tell my parents when I got home. In fact, I didn't mention it until about noon on the day of my birthday. Then, I informed them there would be guests coming at 1 o'clock.

I'm quite certain I never saw my father angrier than he was that afternoon. He said that there would be no party and that moreover, since I had started it, when the kids arrived, I needed to meet them at the door and let them know I hadn't gotten permission for a party and that they couldn't stay.

The worst part, for a person turning eight that day, was that I couldn't accept the gifts they brought.

Never again did I request a birthday party. However, the guys in my dorm made sure I had a special one for my 18th when I was a freshman in college.

*

There was a financial side to my family of which I was completely unaware. I attribute it to our lack of communication. It might have taken longer than the second semester of my freshman year at the University of Illinois for me to start to get a clue had one of my roommates not asked me how much in college loans I expected to graduate with.

I knew I hadn't signed any loan papers, but I also knew I had no idea how my tuition and board was being paid.

My mother explained that they were taking care of the cost because that's what parents do. I thought that meant they were borrowing money, which I didn't want them to do. She told me no, they had been saving and sacrificing for years.

Why hadn't this ever been discussed? I would have gladly agreed to work my way through college – which I ultimately did anyway to have spending money and to buy a car – if it would have meant some family trips during my childhood.

Maybe the answer was for the same reason that I learned about my father being a Bronze Tablet Scholar from the UI, the first one ever from Mahomet. One day between my classes, I had extra time and was walking through the graduate library taking note of the yearly plaques and the names listed that were recognizing the academically honored graduates.

On the 1943 plaque was the name, James C. Kroner.

Questions to my parents were usually answered if I knew which ones to ask. My mother told me that was something they agreed not to mention because they didn't want me to feel pressure to duplicate what they had done.

I was immediately confused because I knew my mother hadn't gone to college.

What "they" was she talking about, I wondered.

"I was the valedictorian of my high school class," she said.

That was two big pieces of family news that I learned the same day.

Even bigger was something I had found out back when I was a high school freshman.

I usually did well in most of my classes, with the exception of science. I didn't like the subject and I'm sure the feeling was mutual.

One day, my freshman general science teacher, Elden Hitchens, said I should go home and ask my father to help me with some of the concepts I just wasn't understanding.

I literally laughed at him, reminding him that my father was a farmer and what would he know about science. I think I actually said, "what would he know about stupid science?"

Mr. Hitchens suggested I ask him that question, too.

I did, primarily so I could have the satisfaction the next day of telling my teacher, "I told you so."

That night, I learned my father's degree from the UI was in

Fred Kroner and Jim Kroner, August, 2000.

chemistry and that he had been recruited by the government immediately after graduation to work on the Manhattan Project. He started by doing research on small reactors and then devoted two years to studying uranium/plutonium isotopes, developing ways to isolate them so they were usable.

I had to tell Mr. Hitchens that my father was a big help. Subsequently, I learned more about my father's role helping to create the first Atomic Bomb, though he talked with reluctance and seldom shared many actual details other than to confirm his involvement.

One reason I was able to get my UI coursework done in eight semesters was that I arranged my schedule with electives in areas other than science.

Sometimes the apple does fall far, far away from the tree.

I graduated from the UI completely debt-free and with a better understanding – but not necessarily a better appreciation – of my parents.

As an adult, I learned that neither of my parents ever had a credit card. The only purchases they would make were ones for which the cash was in the bank. I said surely that didn't include the labor and materials for the new house we moved into in 1960, and my mother said, yes, it did include that.

She said also when my father purchased an additional 60 acres of land early in my teen-age years – to bring his total holdings up close to 300 acres – he paid cash for that as well.

When I was told this, I could only shake my head, knowing that in my wallet were three or four credit cards that were almost always filled to near their maximum limit.

As an aside, when my son Devin went to Rhema Bible College, in Tulsa, Okla., from 2002-05, I made certain he didn't leave with any student-loan debts to repay. After all, that's what families do. Or so I had been told.

My first week in the dorm at the UI more than matched

the number of nights I had spent away from my own bedroom in my entire life.

In the mid-1960s, we went to a family Christmas dinner at Crawfordsville, Ind., on a Sunday. It was at the home of my aunt and uncle, Vera and Lewis Cleek. While there, a snowstorm swept through the area and we heard radio and TV reports that large sections of Interstate 74 were closed.

My family hadn't planned on staying, but did so for one night out of concern for our safety.

A few years later, in 1967, the blizzard of the century roared through Central Illinois. Our rural home was without power for most of the week. When the snow plow made it down our country road, the piles of snow on the sides were in excess of 12 feet. After a couple days, we went into town and stayed with my aunt and uncle, Carol and Don Turner, for three nights.

Each was a weeknight and I absolutely loved getting out of school at 3:15, walking to their house and arriving by 3:20. It beat the heck out of riding the bus until 4:30 each day.

I'm telling you, my friends in town had it good. I could have gotten used to that existence and lifestyle.

Maybe I wouldn't have even wanted or needed a brother or a sister. Maybe.

Besides the two days in Indiana, I was only out of the state of Illinois one other time before college, and it was for just a partial day.

We had relatives on my father's side (the Burwells), whom I had never seen, and we drove to Wellsville, Mo., one summer day in the mid-1960s for a birthday or anniversary celebration. I felt like I knew them because Clara Burwell and Dorothy Burwell always wrote the newsiest letters and included them in their Christmas cards.

They would catch everyone up on all their family highlights

from the previous 12 months. I'm pretty sure my parents just sent cards that said, "Happy holidays."

Fred's Favorites

FAVORITE AUTHORS
1. Mitch Albom
2. Rick Reilly
2. Erle Stanley Gardner
4. John Steinbeck
5. Jim Murray
6. Clair Bee

CHAPTER TEN

During my newspaper career, I had the privilege of working at four daily papers in Central Illinois: Champaign-Urbana Morning Courier, Springfield State-Journal Register, Bloomington Daily Pantagraph and the Champaign-Urbana News-Gazette.

Fred Kroner in The News-Gazette Pressroom,
September, 2013

I worked with – and observed – numerous sports editors before finally becoming one in the final few years of my tenure at The Gazette.

Though others shared the title before me, most didn't share similar views on how to do the job.

At The Courier, Lon Eubanks was the person in charge of the department all four years I was employed there. He was the beat writer for both the University of Illinois football and basketball teams, even completing a book on the history of Illini football while I was on staff.

Eubanks left many of the details of the day-to-day operations to others, notably Dave French.

I learned early that French meant business when he barked an order. One Friday night, after returning to the office from a football game, I was struggling beyond belief to start my story on the Centennial High School contest.

I finally decided to write the body of the story, to buy time to come up with a creative beginning. We wrote our stories using manual typewriters then. This was prior to the time the type-written sheets could be fed into a computer and scanned before getting set in type electronically.

Instead, a copy editor would make marks on the paper and send the pages downstairs to typesetters sitting on the ready at their machines. The typesetters needed a steady flow of copy, even on busy nights, so they didn't suddenly have stories coming to them from 10 different reporters simultaneously.

French would keep track of the time the high school correspondents got to their desks. Thirty minutes later, he figured they'd had enough time to be creative.

I was vaguely aware this night of him saying several times, "Kroner, I need your copy." I stayed focused on my story and if I said anything, it was something like, "Soon."

All of a sudden, he was standing behind me, bellowing, "I need your copy now." I told him, "I'm almost done."

He responded, "Wrong. You are done," and proceeded to roll the paper out of my typewriter.

"I'm in the middle of a sentence," I protested.

"Not any more," French said.

"I don't have a good lead yet," I added.

"Too late," he retorted.

I recognized that an argument close to deadline would serve no purpose, so I relented. I'm certain it was one of the worst stories I ever wrote.

I can't call it 'The Worst,' because that one was still a few months away.

That November, of 1975, the Courier sent various staff members to Illinois State University to cover the state championship football games. It was considered a big deal since the playoffs were still in their infancy, having just been implemented the previous fall.

I was assigned the Class 3A game between Metamora and Geneva. I'm sure I received that game because the copy editors knew the earlier start time would give me several hours to come up with a story. Meeting tight deadlines wasn't a strength during my first year of coverage.

Unbeaten Metamora was the dominant team, beating Geneva 25-7 thanks to a strong running attack that featured the exploits of fullback Larry Sommer.

I didn't know it at the time, but Sommer was one of the school's all-time greats, ultimately receiving selection to the Metamora Hall of Fame in 2017. He was named to multiple All-State teams as a senior in 1975 and rushed for nearly 2,000 yards in 13 games for coach John Helmick.

To me, a state championship game was the pinnacle of the season and I desperately wanted my story to be the absolute best I'd written for any game. I had this feeling in spite of knowing that Metamora was nowhere near our circulation area and that probably no one from that community would ever see my article.

I came close to filling a wastebasket that night at the

office on stories I started that I found unsatisfactory before I decided to take a different direction. One idea I discarded was about Sommer shining bright in the fall. You get the picture.

Another was about Metamora securing its undefeated season by overpowering a team from Chicago's western suburbs. Boring.

Hours passed. My frustrations mounted. I wasn't happy with anything I wrote. Finally, I turned in my story and immediately headed home, feeling as defeated as Geneva.

That feeling was magnified the next morning when I opened up the sports section. The Metamora story was placed in a position or prominence on an inside page.

After the headline, the next thing I noticed was the byline: By The Associated Press.

The next time I saw French, he didn't mince words. "Your story wasn't any good," he said, before giving me what he thought was the good news, "but you still get paid just the same for being there."

I made sure to never again suffer the embarrassment of having one of my stories replaced by a wire service report.

***

My time in Springfield was limited to 12 weeks. That was the length of my 1977 internship.

Larry Harnly was the sports editor, but I didn't have many dealings with him directly since my shift started at 4 p.m. and lasted until midnight.

Jim Ruppert, Jim Wildrick and Hal Pilger were the sportswriters I worked with the most.

The most memorable story from that summer occurred one night when I was assigned to be in the office to edit copy and type in the horseracing results from Sportsmen's Park, as well as to handle anything else that might arise.

As it turned out, some high school-related football development became part of the news cycle. One of the Jims asked me to call a few coaches to get their feedback. They gave me names and phone numbers and turned me loose.

I call the first name on the list. It was Lyle Wind. He was the head coach at Springfield Lanphier. It was to be the first time for me to speak to him.

I got him on the phone, identified myself and explained the background of the story I was working on. I asked for his reaction.

The phone went silent. After what seemed like an eternity, I politely asked, "Are you still there?"

His voice was immediately heard, bellowing, "Christ, I'm thinking," he said.

I don't remember anything else he said. I do remember the other sportswriters, upon hearing the story, saying they should have told me a bit about what to expect from the various coaches I was asked to call.

Overall, my time in Springfield was enjoyable even though I was commuting daily from Champaign, routinely getting back to my apartment about 2 a.m. For only that reason, I was thankful when the 60 days had ended.

By default, I became a regular at the Springfield Speedway, then located on the east side of town along Clear Lake Ave. I knew nothing about auto racing, and wouldn't even call myself a fan. I was sure I couldn't fake my way through a story and write about the intricacies involved in changing a car's setup during the course of an evening, so I chose to write about the personalities who were competitors, such as Rick Standridge, from Divernon, and Jim Leka, from Illiopolis.

Best of all, I was able to cover baseball. Springfield had

a summer-league team that called Lanphier Park its home. One of the best players was an outfielder from the University of Missouri-St. Louis, Grayling Tobias. A year later, he was a 14th-round draft choice by the Montreal Expos.

Tobias was a personable young man, and fun to talk with, but I was most impressed that he was a high-level two-sport athlete in college. He also played basketball. Years later, he was enshrined in his college's Hall of Fame.

The summer of '77 was the first for me to receive a press pass to a major league baseball game. Harnly enjoyed the St. Louis Cardinals, which was fine with me.

The only reason to ever go to a game in St. Louis, in my opinion, is the easy access to the stadium off the interstate, but I will concede, that is a major plus.

I asked for credentials to see the Cubs at Wrigley Field. The agreement was that I could write feature stories about the players, but to let the wire service provide the content for games.

That was the perfect scenario for me. Nothing was better than spending a pregame sitting on the tarp down the left field line with catcher Randy Hundley. I was sitting to his right one day while batting practice was going on. As he spoke, he had his eye on the batters at home plate.

He had obviously been through this drill before.

"Look out," he yelled at one point.

Before I could react, he reached around me and, with his bare hand, stopped a ball which was heading in my direction. He held onto it until the interview ended. Then he flipped it to me.

"Souvenir," he said in his strong Virginia drawl as he walked away.

My first full-time stop in newspapering was in Bloomington.

I considered myself lucky to receive the job offer. The

final semester of my senior year at Illinois, I had numerous projects to finish up at school as well as working at The Courier close to full-time hours, covering everything Centennial.

Bottom line: I was too busy to get resumes printed until March and was way too busy to send out more than one by the time of graduation in May.

That one went to Jim Barnhart, the veteran sports editor at The Pantagraph.

Even though the two professors I had for most of my classes that year – Glenn Hanson and Dick Hildwein – emphasized in class more often that I could count that there were more students enrolled in journalism classes across the country than there were full-time positions at daily newspapers, I wasn't worried.

That's not ego talking, but reality. I was in solid with The Courier and though there were no full-time openings available, French told me I had a part-time job as long as I wanted it.

My plan was to get through the semester at school, relax a bit, then research newspapers and do a resume blitz during the middle of the summer.

Barnhart changed that plan.

He asked me over to interview for an opening.

It was my first in-person interview ever for a job and I didn't have a good handle on how it went.

Until I got home.

The red light on my telephone answering machine was blinking. I listened to the message. It was left by Barnhart, offering me a job.

He needed me to start on May 22, he said, if I was interested. My graduation ceremony was scheduled for May 20.

The exact day the offer was extended is no longer clear, but I know it was late April.

In addition to completing the semester and not letting anything slip at The Courier, I now had to find a place to live in a new town. There was less than a month.

Nonetheless, I took the offer.

Telling my colleagues at The Courier was the toughest goodbye I've ever had to make. Even harder than when I retired from The Gazette because it was a new experience for me.

Turns out – in some respects – it was the best decision I could have made. Less than 10 months after I left, on March 31, 1979, the Morning Courier published its last edition, leaving Champaign-Urbana with one daily newspaper.

At The Daily Pantagraph, I was with a sports editor who was active in all phases of the operation. Barnhart did all of the scheduling, he assigned stories and he covered Illinois State University football and basketball. He didn't do the page layout or edit the stories, but believe me, he read every word once they were printed.

It didn't take me long to learn the extent of his involvement. We had an office bulletin board where schedules and other notes were posted.

I arrived one Saturday afternoon to see red marks on a page torn out of that day's paper. I glanced and realized it was a story I had written. Highlighted was a mistake I had made. It was underlined in red crayon with the phrase, also written in red, "Egads, a fifth-grader would get this right."

I was the first in the office that day and took comfort in thinking my co-workers hadn't seen this. I ripped it off the board and threw it away.

Bad plan.

The following Monday, I was called into a one-on-one

meeting with Barnhart. He asked if I knew what had happened to the note that he posted on the bulletin board.

I told him I'd come in on Saturday, saw it, and took it down, adding that I was sorry about the mistake and would try to be more careful.

He didn't care about my regrets.

"That is my bulletin board," he said. "I put stuff up and I take it down. No one else."

As I left the office, I noticed the bulletin board. He had re-posted the page, with the same red crayon marks and the same comment written in red.

This wasn't something he did to target me. He was an equal-opportunity poster. It didn't matter what the mistake was or who had made it. He pointed it out.

I liked that he wanted us to seek perfection, but I certainly didn't care for his methods.

I worked there for 33 months and didn't keep track of how many times my stories made the board. I'd be lying if I said the first time was also the last time though.

I do know this. To my knowledge, there was only one mistake I made – a typo – that he overlooked or missed. Perhaps it was because it was in agate (the small-type results section usually known as the sports scoreboard).

It was during track season one spring and we were flooded with results of at least a dozen meets. Each time, we had to type in the names of the events since we didn't have a template to use.

Ever notice on your keyboard that the letters "I" and "o" are next to each other? Well, one day in the track and field results section The Daily Pantagraph published what was listed as results for the 'shit put.'

With all of the other crap Barnhart posted, I'll never know how he missed that one.

I found Bloomington-Normal to be much like my college home from the previous years, Champaign-Urbana, and I could have been happy staying there for years.

One of my all-time favorite people I met while in this profession, Bill Flick, got his start as a Pantagraph sportswriter. He had a way of looking at things in a way the average person didn't see.

I swear he could write a riveting story about watching paint dry. He had a personality and sense of humor that drew people in. You always wanted to be in his presence. Never a dull moment.

He stayed with the newspaper for decades, but switched from sports to editorial page columnist and eventually the humorist.

I couldn't stay, however. If it was just the crayon scribblings, perhaps.

There were other, let's say, moral issues, I couldn't overlook.

In the 1970s, in addition to providing newspapers with credentials for the various state tournament games, the IHSA also gave complimentary tickets to those in the news media.

More than once, Pantagraph sportswriters were sent to Champaign – then the yearly home of the state basketball tournaments – in March with a batch of tickets to sell. Barnhart wanted half of the money and he let whoever was covering the games split the remainder.

One time, Mark Wellwood and I decided to "buy" the tickets ourselves. In other words, we calculated what the face value was and split half the cost to give to our sports editor. If we came back unsuccessful, we were chastised for not trying hard enough.

During my third year at The Pantagraph, I started thinking about an exit plan. I hadn't made much movement when a solution unexpectedly presented itself.

***

Tom Reitmann, from The News-Gazette, called me. I knew most of their sports staff, from covering games together with them over the years, and was good friends with several, including Joe Millas and Jean McDonald.

Loren Tate was still the sports editor at The Gazette, but Reitmann was the person who oversaw the operations. He did the hiring.

This time, I didn't need to wonder how I fared in the interview. Reitmann offered me the job while I was at the office, then located at 48 E. Main, in Champaign. Tate wasn't even in the office the day I interviewed.

I told Reitmann I needed time to think about it, but I really didn't.

The next day, I gave two weeks' notice. On March 10, 1981 I started my dream job.

I had grown up reading both The News-Gazette and The Courier, devouring every sports story each day. Being recruited to join the staff was better than any Christmas presents I'd ever received.

Reitmann didn't give me much time to get settled. During the first week – my second day on the job – he tossed me an Illinois men's gymnastics media guide as I got to my desk to start my 4 p.m. shift.

"Read up," he said. "I've got an interview scheduled with the coach for you at 4:30."

I had a decent background on many sports, but gymnastics wasn't one of them. I had never seen a meet in person, nor had I ever interviewed a gymnastics coach or competitor. I wasn't even aware of where the team held its practices.

I glanced quickly at the bio for coach Yoshi Hayasaki, an icon on the UI campus.

Then I made my way to the afternoon practice at Kenney Gym. Let's just say if I had been on a one-day probationary period and judged solely on the story I produced that one day, it would have been a short tenure at the newspaper.

Gracious as he was, I never heard a complaint from Hayasaki. He was probably just elated to get some coverage for the team.

Reitmann was the first of four sports editors I worked under at The Gazette before I was finally given the reins.

Following him were Paul Walsh, Jean McDonald and Jim Rossow. Though I interviewed for most of those other openings, I had no quarrel with the hiring of McDonald or Rossow. They were examples of being promoted from within and I was especially fond of that policy.

Eventually, it worked to my benefit, too.

Walsh was brought in from the outside and was somebody I liked best when he was gone, but not the way it sounds.

In retrospect, I recognized what he was trying to do, not only with me, but also with the entire staff. Of any editor I worked with at daily newspapers, Walsh was far and away the leader for editing copy, working with reporters on rewrites and suggesting changes to make the copy stronger. Sometimes he didn't suggest. He insisted.

I was not yet 30 years old when he arrived and had the mentality that everything I wrote was fine as is and didn't need adjustments. With experience, you come to realize that any story can be improved, if you put the effort into it.

We butted heads a few times, but I guarantee that every one of my stories that he didn't just blindly accept was improved after listening to him and making the revisions.

Walsh also demonstrated a loyalty to his writers. He would criticize when he felt he needed to, but he would bend over backwards with his support when he thought it was warranted.

Of all the dreams and expectations I had for myself as a writer – to write books, to cover the Cubs, to write songs –

never once did I think, "have a series of stories nominated for a Pulitzer Prize."

And yet, it happened. Thanks to Paul Walsh.

In 1985, I wrote a series of newspaper stories detailing and discussing high school athletes using drugs. They weren't unnamed athletes doing unnamed things. They were former athletes from around Champaign-Urbana who were willing to share their stories while authorizing use of their names.

I was told a story about an athlete carrying speed in his sock during a game (told by the athlete himself) and then using the halftime break to go to the restroom and take a hit.

Walsh wanted to make sure that no one recanted after the fact and denied they spoke to me. He made sure each of the former athletes came to the office and signed a piece of paper granting permission for his name to be used. Walsh was in the conference room with me as an added witness as the paper was signed.

The stories sent shock waves through the community. People were surprised to hear that these things were taking place locally.

Walsh sent an equal shock through me the day he said he had convinced The News-Gazette Board of Directors to authorize the necessary payment to submit my stories to the Pulitzer committee.

I received a letter back stating that the entry had been accepted.

That, in itself, made me feel like a winner.

Walsh left soon thereafter and was replaced by Jean McDonald, whom I had first met as we were going through the UI together.

She was the absolute best ever at organizing everything in the department and had been doing so long before her promotion. Dismayed that The Associated Press produced weekly state polls for high school football and boys' basketball teams in the state, but nothing for girls' sports, she single-handedly got statewide polls started for volleyball and girls' basketball.

The AP agreed to send the polls to all of its members, but they had no intention of conducting the polls.

McDonald handled it herself, arranging for 16 coaches in each class to make weekly calls to The News-Gazette. Actually, they called twice each week.

The first time was to get updates on results – remember, this was pre-Internet and scores weren't readily available – and the second was to cast their votes.

I was her right-hand man on this project and that's how I got to interact with some of the all-time state greats, such as Chicago's Dorothy Gaters, the winningest basketball coach in state history.

McDonald brought those talents to her job as sport editor and I'm sure we had more staff meetings during her tenure than in all the other years I worked combined. That was a good thing. Everyone knew what was going on, what was coming up and what was expected.

Her departure to teach at the UI was a blessing for the journalism students who would enroll at the college, but a loss for the newspaper even though she had shifted from sports to information technology in her final years with The Gazette.

Jim Rossow came into the editor's job next and, like all others, left his imprint in many ways.

He has a charisma that is hard to ignore and has a more thorough knowledge and understanding of the newspaper business than anyone with whom I've been associated.

He oversaw the transition of the paper from the traditional printed pages to a larger online presence, the social media segment, first in sports and then when he became the newspaper editor, with the entire publication.

He insisted that we do podcasts, blogs and videos. We posted content on Facebook. He wanted to increase our visibility for those who relied on technology to get information. We tweeted updates from the games we covered. More than any other person, Rossow is responsible for The News-Gazette consistently being among the top newspapers nationally for its circulation.

His vision is uncanny and his decisions spot-on. There's no wondering why The Gazette was annually recognized as one of the country's top sports sections. Yes, we had a good crew, but we had an even better leader who could get the best out of everyone. And, he could do so as the staff size was shrinking and the responsibilities on those remaining were increasing.

When he asked you to do something, it wasn't really a question with two possible answers. He was persuasive, but never in an under-handed manner. Someone once said he could sell ice to an Eskimo.

I believe it.

Eighteen months after I officially retired from The Gazette, Rossow called late one afternoon. He had something so exciting to talk to me about, he said, that he had to see me in person. It was too big to discuss on the phone.

I made – and kept – an appointment. Once again, I was offered a job without applying.

The editor position was opening up at my hometown newspaper, The Mahomet Citizen, which is one of the weeklies under The Gazette's umbrella.

He wanted me to take over as editor.

I was reluctant.

"Think about it," he said.

"You're perfect for the job," he said.

"There's no one better," he said.

I was still reluctant.

"You don't have to tell me today," he said.

I wound up taking the job and enjoyed all aspects of it.

Except one.

I was not only Editor, I was Everything.

I answered the phones, took payments for new subscriptions or renewals, looked into why customers weren't getting their papers, hired correspondents, assigned stories and edited their submissions, took pictures, determined general page layouts and locked the door at night. When I wasn't in the office, no one was.

And, of course, I interviewed folks and wrote about a dozen stories a week.

In short, it evolved into more work for the weekly than I ever did in a week for the daily. And, I had some pretty long days/nights with the daily. My ex-wives will vouch for that.

I gave up The Citizen job after nine months and walked into what was truly a dream retirement job as a freelance correspondent for the online Mahomet Daily.

Once again, I didn't submit an application. I wonder how many other people, with 50-plus years of experience and multiple locations worked, have only applied for one full-time job?

It will be my final job, not a stepping stone into something bigger and better. This is plenty big, and really good.

If I could extract the best traits of all the editors I've worked with for decades and place them into one individual, it would be with the visionary who started the Mahomet Daily from scratch in 2013, Dani Tietz.

She is demanding from the standpoint of expecting quality, accurate work and stories that aren't fluff pieces, but which have meaning, substance and relevance.

She is not demanding from the standpoint of making a

staggering amount of assignments and expecting completed works in an unreasonable amount of time.

Instead, it's a work environment where you feel like you can breathe and have a life between stories. Deadlines are fluid. Story lengths are fluid.

The first time an editor told me to "write what you want," was the last time until I became part of the Mahomet Daily team. I may not be able to create an edible meat loaf, but I can create a story – on any subject – of any length and keep a reader's interest until the final word.

The best part of the association with Dani Tietz is the freedom to pursue stories I find of particular interest. She'll make suggestions, but isn't offended if I turn some down. Likewise, she doesn't act like I am usurping her authority when I suggest story possibilities.

I had grown accustomed to finding my own story ideas.

Starting in 1991, I had a unique arrangement at The Gazette.

That year, The Gazette opened a bureau in Danville whose sole purpose was to produce a Vermilion County morning edition Monday through Friday.

Just months prior to the formation of this bureau, I had moved into a just-built country home north of Mahomet and wasn't anxious to relocate. It was on farm land which had been in the family for decades. John Foreman, the long-time News-Gazette editor and publisher, convinced me that this was the job I wanted.

Then he sweetened the deal unlike any cake I have ever tasted. And, that's too many to count!

"If you take this job," Foreman said, "you can strictly be a writer and get out of all desk shifts except one each year (everyone was required to work one holiday desk shift annually)."

There are people who excel in the office, writing headlines

(Dan Heaton, Mike Goebel, Rich Barak and Tony Mancuso immediately come to mind), creating innovative layouts (Goebel and Don O'Brien, especially) and editing reporters' copy (Heaton, Barak and Jason Randall, especially), and then there is me. I'd read the stories all the time wishing I'd been at that event or I'd be thinking about where I was headed the next day. Or, wondering why another coach hadn't returned my call.

Foreman also agreed to pay me mileage for my almost daily trips into Vermilion County since I was unwilling to move. During the 1990s, I put an average of 35,000 miles a year on my car. Vermilion County was a focal point, but I was anywhere between Kankakee and Mattoon as well as between Bloomington and the Indiana state line on a regular basis.

Geographically, we had a huge circulation area. At one time – prior to consolidations and closings – we covered 50 high schools.

As the person in charge of the Vermilion County sports bureau, I only had to answer to myself. I picked the games to cover, the stories to research, the athletes and coaches to profile. It's a freedom I never took for granted as I distributed the coverage throughout the entire area for which I was responsible.

I added innovations that hadn't been done previously, getting the high school perspective from students who would submit a weekly story and then – as the 1990s came to a close – selecting an all-decade team for every sport, both at the high school and the junior college level in Vermilion County.

It's a freedom I have once again with the Mahomet Daily. Dani Tietz has a terrific knack for welcoming and encouraging, for nurturing and pushing, all the while supporting. When stories become a struggle – as they do for everyone who writes – her feedback and perspective allows me to see the picture from a different view, opening up new ways to tell the tale.

It's fitting, like the expression goes, that the best was saved for last.

Fred Kroner talks with the football referee crew prior to a game at Danville High School, October, 2013. The referee with the white cap is Mark Brooks.

Fred Kroner at Kickapoo State Park, covering a cross-country meet.

Fred Kroner on the sidelines at a high school football game.

Fred Kroner interviewing a wheelchair athlete after the Christie Clinic Illinois Marathon at the UI's Memorial Stadium.

Fred Kroner interviewing Mahomet-Seymour senior Christian Romine, March, 2015.

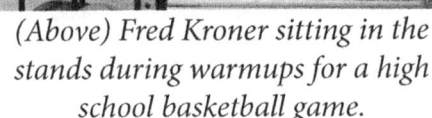

(Above) Fred Kroner sitting in the stands during warmups for a high school basketball game.

Fred Kroner at the UI Assembly Hall, covering the state wrestling tournament in 2014.

Fred Kroner interviewing an unidentified athlete at the girls' state track and field meet, in Charleston.

John Spezia speaks as Fred Kroner listens at Fred's retirement party from The News-Gazette, June, 2015.

CHAPTER ELEVEN

I once told someone that I didn't have a job, I had an adventure.

More than anything, that is what was most enjoyable about the work I did. It was always different.

Forget the fact that no two games are alike, even when the schools are the same and they are playing a rematch.

I had a routine in the fall. Mondays and Wednesdays were generally set aside for interviews. Tuesdays were a day to cover volleyball, Thursdays were for soccer, Fridays for football and Saturdays for cross-country.

The winter didn't offer as much variety as basketball for boys and girls, along with wrestling and swimming, were the only prep choices.

The arrival of spring meant another assortment of events.

It was hard to schedule days for particular sports because the weatherman often didn't cooperate. During a week, I would generally watch a baseball game, a softball game, a track and field meet and – frequently – a girls' soccer match.

As much as I love baseball, I don't think I would have thrived in an environment where I went to Spring Training with a major league team in February, spent the entire summer traveling with the team and then devoted much of the fall to the playoffs.

I loved the challenges of covering the many different sports, and coming in contact with so many different people. I'd rarely run across the same individuals twice in the same week.

We always remember our firsts, right? The first crush. The first home run (OK, OK, the only home run!) The first date.

I vividly recall the first solo byline article I wrote for a newspaper. It was written in the spring of 1975 for the Morning Courier.

It was a feature story on a former major league baseball player who lived in southwest Champaign, Dick Hyde.

It was also my first in-person interview. I was still living in the dorms at the UI and walked to his residence. We had a great conversation, but I'm sure the time I spent getting there and then walking back to my room was greater than the time we talked.

A little more than a decade later, I had the privilege of covering his son, Richard, in baseball when he pitched for Centennial High School.

I also remember that the first byline story I was a part of at The Courier involved my high school alma mater and a controversy that was going on.

As basketball practice was starting for the 1974-75 season, Mahomet-Seymour was only offering the sport for boys. Title IX was in effect, but hadn't been implemented at all school districts in the state.

There was a girl who wanted to play for the Bulldogs, Diane Carper, and she tried out for the boys' team. She didn't make the final cut, but it was a story closely followed by the media. I co-authored some stories in The Courier about it.

By the time M-S formed a girls' varsity basketball program, Carper had graduated and was a few years away from working for the state police.

Not all of my sports memories are from events I covered.

The first year I was at The News-Gazette, my good friend Walter Pierce asked me to help him and Chuck Schwartz coach a Little League baseball team (The Brokers) at Bottenfield School.

I spent five years in this volunteer position, from 1981-85, and met some wonderful young athletes who later became lettermen at various high schools in town. One of our players was an individual I lost track of until 1992, when I discovered that Steve Raquel was Chief Illiniwek.

Fred Kroner and Steve Raquel, whom he coached in Little League, March, 2014.

CHAPTER TWELVE

I wasn't prepared for the question.

"Would you do it again?"

The speaker, this time, was a junior high student.

For some reason, journalists are popular choices to speak to groups of students. For decades, I've been asked to speak to classes from elementary age to ones in college.

I can still remember when and how it started. I was a new hire at The News-Gazette when Allison White, and soon thereafter, Georgine Hembrough, asked me to talk to their respective high school classes at Centennial. I was a regular visitor throughout the 1980s.

Whatever time limit I am given, I always made sure to save at least 10 minutes at the end for questions. I would much rather discuss something that I know is of interest to someone in the group I am addressing.

Sometimes, I would wonder, 'Why bother?'

One of the first elementary school classes I spoke to in the 1990s ended with this question: "What size shoe do you wear?"

The teacher interceded and decided it was time to thank the guest for his time, and that was that.

Another time, in the introduction from the teacher, she explained that I covered a variety of sports and traveled to a variety of locations.

Before I could even say anything, a boy raised his hand. Against my better judgment, I said, "I'll take one question before I tell you about being a sportswriter."

Fred Kroner at Champaign Central, January, 2015, when he received the Distinguished Media Award from the IHSA.

The exact date escapes my mind, but it was in the late-1990s, when the Chicago Bulls were the dominant team in the NBA.

The question: "Do you have Michael Jordan's phone number?"

My friends are often amazed at how many numbers I have in my contact list, but that was never one of them.

And now, back to the morning when a youngster asked a serious question and quietly waited for an answer: "Would you do it again?"

It may seem like an easy question. There are two choices,

right?

Yes.

Or no.

It's not that simple, and knowing that the class period would be ending in a matter of minutes, I couldn't do the question justice in such a short amount of time.

Plus, I'm not sure I have an answer.

My answer was honest, at least as much as I said.

"If I were going back in time, knowing only what I knew in junior high or high school, absolutely I would follow the same path."

The student didn't ask a follow-up, but there is one that begs to be addressed.

Would I do it again, if I knew then what I know now?

Wow. How do you turn your back on a lifetime of work, mostly rewarding work, mostly pleasurable work?

How do you say you would trade watching – and meeting – some of the biggest names in sport for another occupation?

How many bigger names are there in the history of basketball than John Wooden? How many American Olympians have made a bigger impact than Bonnie Blair? How many greater wheelchair marathoners have there been than Jean Driscoll? How many greater athletes have come from Centennial High School than Roger McClendon? From Urbana than Tyke Peacock? From Danville than Keon Clark? From Mahomet-Seymour than Phil Knell? From Oakwood than Darrin Fletcher? From Unity than Brian Cardinal? From Buckley-Loda than Scott Garrelts?

They are all individuals I have interviewed – most multiple times – and they are people I never would have met had I been an accountant, a farmer, a store clerk, a stay-at-home father or virtually anything except a journalist.

Most of the encounters are still prominent in my mind decades after they occurred.

I interviewed Garrelts, then pitching for the San Francisco Giants, in the 1980s on the steps of the visiting dugout at Busch Stadium, in St. Louis. He wasn't scheduled to pitch that day, so I had unlimited pre-game access with the right-hander.

Upon concluding our talk, I used my press pass to access the field as batting practice was about to finish, walked to the Cardinals' dugout and boldly asked manager Whitey Herzog if I could speak to him for a few minutes. He said he was just going back to his office and said if I wanted to join him, I was welcome.

Herzog was as gracious as anyone I've dealt with in professional baseball.

The meeting with Wooden was purely by chance.

In 1984, I spent my own money to travel to Los Angeles for the McDonalds All-American boys' basketball game. Centennial's McClendon was one of the competitors. It was the first time Champaign-Urbana had a representative.

I walked into Pauley Pavilion to watch an afternoon practice. The entrance I took found me at one of the upper levels and I started heading down a series of stairs to reach the floor. After the first flight, I noticed a man to my right sitting by himself.

I hurried past, not wanting to miss the start of the workout. Then, a few steps later, I turned and did a double-take. Based on newspaper and magazine pictures I had seen, I was certain the man was John Wooden, the famed former UCLA head coach.

I decided I had nothing to lose. I approached the man, identified myself and told him I was from Champaign, Ill.

"Another Midwestern," John Wooden said. "I'm from Indiana myself."

We proceeded to talk for the duration of the practice, like

two people who had known one another for years, not for minutes.

I called my sports editor that night and told him I had a sidebar.

"It had better be good," Paul Walsh said.

"How about a feature on John Wooden, who coached 10 NCAA championship teams in a 12-year span?" I responded.

"We'll get a file picture," Walsh said, approvingly.

I was on board with Bonnie Blair when she was still someone trying to establish an identity in a sport – speedskating – that the majority of Americans knew nothing about.

I was one of those.

She tutored me, told me how important dryland training was. She had to also tell me what dryland training was (basically, simulating ice training on land). We would meet for iced tea at the Ground Round, on Neil St., and talk for hours. She shared her dreams, stories about her family, the difficulty of getting ice time at the UI Ice Arena and whatever else was on her mind.

I received one of the first bumper stickers that her local sponsor, the Champaign Police Benevolent Association, put out.

It referred to Blair as "Champaign's favorite speeder." It was more than appropriate after she broke the Olympic 500-meter sprint record.

I'm not sure if that bumper sticker idea was the brainchild of Jerry Schweighart – who eventually became the Champaign mayor – but I know he was involved with the decision.

Over the decades, I'm not sure I found any other families as genuinely nice and reflective as the Blairs. And so appreciative and gracious.

I will make a confession, too. The only time I ever asked for an autograph, it was for Bonnie Blair's. She did better than sign her name on a piece of paper. She had a picture taken with me, had a print made and then signed it.

My only regret was that The News-Gazette never ordered credentials for me to cover any of the Winter Olympic Games. That would have been more spectacular than watching on television.

Blair wasn't the only speedskater of prominence from Champaign-Urbana. Another one whom I had the pleasure to watch compete for years was Erik Henriksen, who years later wound up being a fellow Mahomet resident.

Before I got to know Tyke Peacock, I wondered what this guy was all about. I'd never seen an athlete approach his track events as nonchalant as he did.

While in high school, he would routinely not take his sweats off while competing in the high jump. If the bar reached a certain height, he would then remove the sweat pants.

I questioned how serious he was when I heard how he warmed up for the state meet in Charleston. He went to the indoor fieldhouse adjacent to the track and played basketball. Then, he went outside and won the high jump state championship.

He was terrific in basketball, but world-class as a high jumper. Before I retired from The Gazette, I had the privilege of telling his life's story, the troubling times, the fall from grace, and how he pulled himself up and became clean and sober. It was as much of a success story as about any champion I have covered.

He shared everything, the good and the bad, and didn't try to gloss over the troubled times.

Darrin Fletcher was the only player I've known who could hold his own as a teen-ager in the amateur Eastern Illinois Baseball League. In the early 1980s, many college pitchers –

and recent college pitchers – dotted the rosters of the various E.I. teams.

The left-handed hitting catcher – between stints with an American Legion summer team – maintained a batting average well above .300 while facing crafty pitchers at least six years his senior. It was no surprise he wound up in the major leagues.

Keon Clark was a Danville enigma. A dominating center, he blocked 150 shots as a high school senior for a Vikings' team which placed third at state, but he didn't display the passion for basketball that one would expect for someone with his skills.

In 1998, the 6-foot-11 Clark was the 13th player taken in the NBA Draft. He was selected by the Orlando Magic. I covered a reception, which he attended briefly, at Lincoln Park, in Danville, a site where he had frequently played outdoors as a youngster.

He was always tough to interview because he didn't say a lot. I sensed that he was excited about having an NBA future, but didn't get the impression that it was the highlight of his life at that point.

On the other hand, there was Brian Cardinal. I knew his coach, Don Akers, from his time working in the Mahomet-Seymour school district, and I had multiple occasions to watch Cardinal play.

The way his career ultimately skyrocketed made me realize I never would have made it as a talent scout. At no time – even when he was excelling at Purdue – would I have predicted he'd play in the NBA.

Cardinal is the classic example of not being able to measure heart and desire. I doubt if I ever saw a prep athlete in Central Illinois that could match those traits to his level. He literally willed himself into the career that he had.

He not only made it to the NBA, but had back-to-back seasons where his scoring average was nearly in double figures (9.6 in 2003-04 and 9.0 in 2004-05) and he started games with four different teams.

, a two-time Olympic medalist, willingly shared her story with me during a 1997 interview, confiding what she felt upon learning she would be confined to a wheelchair.

"Now, my life is over," she said.

She talked about everything from severe depression to winning more Boston Marathon races than anyone in history. It's the type of story that serves to give hope to others who face unthinkable adversity and challenges.

Driscoll didn't give up, and she was rewarded. And she talked about issues that she would rather not have made public, but did so because she realized others might benefit.

Phil Knell set the bar high for his athletic achievements at Mahomet-Seymour. A four-year starter in football, he never played in a losing game. His football teams were 32-0.

In track he set school records, and in basketball, his career point total ranks among the all-time leaders more than a half-century after playing in his final game.

He was a charter member when the M-S Education Foundation established a Hall of Fame in 2017 and was honestly delighted to be remembered so many years after his graduation in 1963.

Those people, and those memories, however, don't even come close to filling my list of top memories.

How can you overlook the experience a 23-year-old had on Jan. 11, 1979 when he covered the University of Illinois beating the No. 1-ranked Michigan State University men's basketball team, 57-55, on a baseline jumper by Eddie Johnson?

The game attracted so much national media attention that the Bloomington Daily Pantagraph – where I worked at the time – was assigned special seating in the auxiliary boxes in the top row of the C-section so that the national media could have the ideal spots in the regular press box. I didn't mind the location, but can't say the same about the reporters who joined me with having to fight our way through the crowds afterwards to get to the floor for the postgame press conference.

The press conference started when the national media was all assembled, not when all of the reporters were present in the room.

A decade later, working for The News-Gazette, I was in Phoenix to visit my high school friend, Rick Durst. The Phoenix Suns had a home game that night, but I made arrangements to meet up with Eddie Johnson after a morning shootaround.

That was one of two memories from the weekend. It was also the first time I saw a cotton field in person. I pulled my rental car off to the side of the road to get an up-close look.

Johnson, meanwhile, took me to the deepest depths of the arena – it seemed like we were a mile underground – and we chatted until all the others, including the coaches and trainers, had left the building. He wasn't in a hurry, or if he was, he didn't show it.

For every bad story that's reported about how ungrateful and uncooperative professional athletes are, you run across "winners" such as Eddie Johnson, who deserves a place on anyone's all-interview team.

Johnson played in nearly 1,200 NBA games during his illustrious 17-year-career and scored more than 19,000 points. The two points I remember most are from his college career and made headlines nationally.

So, why the hesitation about whether I would do it again?

Call me naïve, but when I considered the profession, it never crossed my mind that most games are played outside the normal 8 a.m.-5 p.m. work shift.

For fans, evening games are ideal. They are finished with their work days and the games provide an occasional outing. For those who cover the games, especially at the high school level where there is something practically every night except Sunday, it often means being away from a spouse who works all day, and a child who is in school during the day.

Anyone can make that schedule work for a short period of time. I tried to make it work for nearly 40 years and three marriages.

The original appeal to the job was combining sports and writing. As I retired, the interest in writing had not waned at all, but I had morphed into one of the biggest non-sports fans around.

Since the turn of the century, I've watched seven full baseball games and all of them were during the 2016 World Series. The last NBA game I watched in full was when Michael Jordan was playing. The only NFL game I watch each year is the Super Bowl and, truly, one of the highlights that night are the commercials.

When you are surrounded by something every day – and I do mean EVERY day – such as I was with sports, there is a need to get away from it once at home and in my non-working hours. By the time I retired, I was so far away from being a "fan," that I didn't consider changing my ways.

I'll watch an occasional Illini football or basketball game, but that's it. Although I will confess, I check the box scores for Cubs' games multiple times a day or night.

Journalists are drilled, from the time we're in school, "no cheering in the press box."

It's a good policy, certainly, but something that is hard to turn on and off.

My son, Devin, played youth soccer for eight years, and had more than his share of highlights, but it never seemed right for me to cheer. Most of the time I watched as a neutral spectator would instead of the way a proud father would.

I was always beaming on the inside.

I've transitioned from a person who knew the batting order for every National League team in the 1960s to someone who now can't associate many player names with their teams, unless they happen to play for the Cubs.

I'm thankful that I don't need to go back in time and use my current knowledge to pick a profession for my life. My decisions were made already and I have to live with those choices.

I also don't know what viable alternative I would have had. I'm not a fix-up or repair guy. Anything involving sales would not be appealing. Nor can I see myself as an accountant or a banker.

The closest I could come, I think, would be in education. But somehow, when I think about teaching, I wonder how often I would get irrelevant questions like, "What size shoe do you wear?"

CHAPTER THIRTEEN

Covering high school sports in Central Illinois for me meant going beyond the boundaries of the 11 counties where area schools were located.

Two of the most memorable ventures occurred in the summer of 1994 and the summer of 1995.

Dan Park, the personable girls' basketball coach at Hoopeston Area, orchestrated exchange trips to Beijing in 1994 and to Sydney, Australia, a year later. He worked with a reputable company, International Sports Exchange.

The first trip included 14 girls' basketball players and 11 volleyball players from Central Illinois. Shawn Lane, from Milford, and Beth Carpenter, from Hoopeston, served as the volleyball coaches.

Park, who was in charge of the basketball team, invited me along as a reporter to chronicle the trip on a daily basis for the folks back home.

I later learned he needed an additional chaperone, too.

As often happens in travel, the getting from here to there eventually overshadowed the games that were played in China.

Our entourage was scheduled on a flight from Indianapolis

to San Francisco. More than half of the reservations on the first leg of the flight had been deleted, causing major headaches and havoc trying to keep the entire group together.

Park knew where to place the blame on that June morning, 1994.

"People make mistakes," he said, "but if you really want to screw it up, use a computer."

We arrived in San Francisco and prepared for the 15-hour flight to Beijing. There were more than 300 passengers on Air China Flight 986 and we departed on time.

The story I filed for the June 22, 1994 News-Gazette started like this:

"Day one.

"One day to remember.

"One day best forgotten."

Twenty-two minutes into the flight, our plane turned back. Much of the conversation took place in Chinese – and we didn't yet have our interpreter – so we didn't have a good understanding of the situation.

However, we assumed it to be serious when we looked out the windows on either side as we touched down and saw the runway lined with fire trucks and ambulances with lights flashing.

The next day's edition of the San Francisco Chronicle provided a few details, noting, engine No. 2 on Air China Flight 986 "flamed out and had to be shut down."

Many of the teen-aged girls were willing to forego the remainder of the trip in lieu of returning home or making other plans.

"I don't want to go to China anymore," Milford setter Shannon Garrelts said. "Maybe stay here in California and go shopping."

A day later, the mood became even more sour. We returned to the airport and sat through two delays before being told the trip was being postponed another 24 hours. In a test flight, a problem was discovered in a second engine.

Needless to say, our collective confidence level in this trip having a positive outcome was low.

"Maybe we should take this as a sign we weren't supposed to go," Danville basketball player LaTana Lillard said.

The good news is that the airline provided food vouchers and free lodging at the local Hyatt, which was offset by all passengers being unable to retrieve their checked bags. Some of us were wearing the same clothes on Thursday as we were when we left Indianapolis on Tuesday.

Some of the group washed garments in the hotel sinks and used hair dryers to dry them.

Behind the scenes, the official delegate assigned to us by International Sports Exchange was working to extend the trip by two days since our departure time from San Francisco was now set at 52 hours after the original flight time.

This didn't make everyone happy. Carpenter was planning on a July 1 return so she could attend her 20-year high school class reunion on July 2. Lillard was among the athletes who had commitments with a summer team immediately after the scheduled return date.

Ultimately, the 10-day trip did become a 12-day trip.

We successfully landed in Beijing at 1 a.m. local time and learned that the hosts who were to pick us up had left because their work day had ended. It was 4 a.m. before we finally arrived at the hotel.

The good news is that everyone's luggage arrived.

The bad news is that both the volleyball and basketball teams had games scheduled less than 12 hours after our arrival. The schedule was established in advance, originally with two days to relax and sightsee first, but the delayed arrival eliminated that option.

For the Central Illinois athletes – and the sportswriter –

the first volleyball game started at what would have been 2 a.m. back home. The opening basketball game felt like 3 a.m.

I soon had my own set of frustrations. My daily stories had to be submitted by fax, which only became a problem when my two-page filings were charged at a different rate each of the first three days in the country.

I had our interpreter look into it and his answer surprised me: "It depends on the time you send the fax," he said.

In retrospect, my memories are not so much about the games – though the basketball team was 4-0 – but of what we observed. Parking lots were filled with rows and rows of bicycles.

Little children who couldn't have been more than 6 or 7 were begging for money daily, looking pleadingly at us and saying, "Mister, please."

One day, en route to one of the gymnasiums, our bus driver was pulled over. We don't know what was said, but at one point, he reached into a storage compartment, pulled out a carton of cigarettes, handed them to the officer and then – after the two men shook hands – we were back on the road again.

When we ate at restaurants, we were always shuttled into a separate banquet-type room, which prevented us from interacting with the locals.

We were encouraged to barter for goods we saw at street shops. I was not successful at all. Some of our group wished they hadn't done as well.

Rachel Wilson, from Rossville-Alvin, found an item she wanted. It was listed at 660 yuan (approximately $83). She made the purchase for 200 yuan (approximately $25).

Afterwards, she said, "That's probably the only time I'll do that. I feel bad about it."

The 1995 trip to Sydney was a memorable one for me.

I took advantage and brought along my 12-year-old son, Devin, with me. It was fun to experience the adventure with him. We got to throw boomerangs at a working ranch, we got to hold a koala bear at the zoo and we got to see some of the venues that were under construction already for the 2000 Olympics.

The best part? When I needed time back at the motel to write my daily reports, there were about 15 teen-aged girls willing to serve as babysitters as they splashed around the pool.

Park took a girls' basketball team again that year, but the volleyball coaches didn't return. In the areas where we visited in Australia, all high schools which offered swimming had outdoor pools.

The memories were priceless and I'm delighted that I used my vacation time each summer to participate in what were truly once-in-a-lifetime experiences. I've never been back to either country.

It was also an opportunity to see these young people in a different way than merely as athletes in their sports.

Many of these people, such as Milford's Shannon Garrelts and Tuscola's Andrea Wax (who was on the trip to Australia), later became lifelong friends.

Another trip of note took place in 2002. There were no area athletes involved and no stories to file for the newspaper.

John Spezia, the Hall of Fame basketball coach who spent years at Danville Area Community College, was involved with a series of clinics in Antigua. He invited myself and WDAN general manager Mike Hulvey to accompany him – along with our spouses – and spend time mentoring local journalists about covering the sport.

Our motel accommodations were fouled up. The Hulveys and the Spezias wound up in an older motel in the city. My wife Emily and I were given a room in a new, but rural, resort. Our expected time of socializing and enjoying each other's company never materialized.

We were also in an open-air room, which sounds nice in theory. However, when one of us – me – is a mosquito magnet and the netting which management provided was ineffective, my body was soon a mass of bumps that required scratching. I couldn't wait to get on the plane for home.

One of my most enjoyable summers was 1990.

At different times, the IHSA has had a variety of rules and regulations governing high school teams and summer camps or games. At one time, the coaches could be involved, but not more than two players from any team could make up the roster.

Later, entire teams could stay together, but the coach could have no role in the games.

Later yet, coaches were given a number of contact days – 25 – that they could work with their athletes in the summer, whether as a group at a camp or in a summer league, or individually at their schools.

In 1990, teams could compete as one, but the high school coach could not be involved.

I had gotten to know the Sullivan High School girls' basketball head coach, Scott Thomas. He was one of the most committed and dedicated coaches I have known, regardless of sport.

He would routinely go home immediately after a game, watch the video, chart the stats and then call in his statistics. This was before our deadlines were moved to 10 p.m. and we had all night to finish stories, as long as they were done by the time the morning crew arrived at 6 a.m.

I was typically one of the last sportswriters out of the office – though I had serious competition in the mid-1980s when Jeff Pierron was on staff – and was curious when our red sports hotline phone would break the silence around 3 a.m. with its insistent ringing.

I didn't know what to expect the first time I answered.

"Hello. This is Coach Thomas. Is there someone there who can take the results from our game?" the voice on the other end asked.

I was accommodating and was naturally curious as to why he picked that time to call.

"I just finished watching the film and charting the stats," he said. "I like to do that myself to make sure they are accurate."

I, too, have a penchant for accuracy in statistics, and it was the start of a lasting friendship. Some nights, if I knew his Redskins had played a game, I would delay leaving the office until I got his call because I had so much respect for his approach.

As the 1989-90 basketball season was ending, Thomas mentioned an idea he had been considering. He needed someone to coach his team in the summer, but he made it clear he didn't really want that someone to do much coaching.

What he was seeking was someone to be on the bench, overseeing the group, filling out the lineup sheets and making substitutions. He wanted the players to work through situations on their own rather than have a coach call a timeout and instruct them what to do.

"I'm sure you could get parent volunteers," I said.

I figured there would be plenty who would attend their children's summer activities anyway and would be delighted to help out.

Thomas was resistant to that idea. He explained that once parents get involved in that manner, they feel like they have ownership in the program and when the school year comes around can – and should – offer input and be heard.

The high school team was going to be Thomas' and he would make the decisions without any interference from outside sources. He knew I wouldn't be one to second-guess his strategies, so I could be trusted to sit on the bench for the summer season.

What ultimately led to my decision to accept the volunteer position was the desire to write a story about the experience. I liked to do first-person articles like this.

The previous summer, I signed up for the horseshoe competition in the Prairie State Games and turned the afternoon of competition into a column. Years later, I journeyed over to Indiana where everyday people had a chance to drive a race car around a track for a few laps. (It wasn't bad when I was on the track by myself, going over 100 mph, but it was nerve-wracking when others got on the track before I completed my run. And, I gained a new appreciation for the shoulder strength needed to guide the car where you wanted it to go.)

The Sullivan girls' basketball team had a full summer schedule in 1990. It required creative use of my vacation time to get to everything. There was a summer league at Jamaica High School, another one in Mattoon, a tournament at Ridgeview High School and team camps at Illinois State University and – the grand finale – an elite team camp at Bradley University.

It was at the Bradley camp where the girls gave me a nickname that they still mention a quarter of a century later: The Mad Statter.

The last part is obvious. I always charted every statistic imaginable at games and within seconds after a game ended – without the help of a computer – could tell someone how many offensive rebounds they had or how many turnovers the team had or the time on the clock when the team took the lead for good.

One afternoon, while coaching and charting stats simultaneously, one of the referees made a disgustingly terrible call (imagine that?) and I apparently threw down my clipboard harder than I intended. It shattered into multiple pieces, I'm sure because it was an older one I had used for many years.

It was either Amanda Glazebrook or Becky Clayton that began referring to me as The Mad Statter.

The Bradley Camp was ultimately the one I focused on in my July 4, 1990 column in The News-Gazette.

It started like this:

"With apologies to Duke's Mike Krzyzewski, there's another Coach K along the sidelines.

"At least there was during the weekend.

"A sportswriter whose thinking parallels that of many Americans (it can't be THAT hard) took a seat on the bench for last weekend's USA Basketball elite girls' team camp at Bradley University, in Peoria."

The team had already won the Ridgeview tournament as well as the ISU team camp, but the 14-team field at Bradley consisted of many of the top projected teams in several states for the upcoming year, both in Class 1A and Class 2A."

As the column continued, I wrote:

"How can you ever really be ready for something you've never done before?

"Soon, as the time for the first scheduled game drew nearer, one question automatically led to another.

"Will they listen?" was replaced by, "Why should they listen?

"Will Coach K do the right thing?" was replaced by, "What is the right thing?

"Will this lead to a career change?" was replaced by "How

did Coach K get convinced to do this?"

The Sullivan team beat a school from St. Louis by eight points in the tournament opener.

I wrote:

"Coach K executed his game plan to perfection: to always have five players on the floor. It was only a temporary situation when Sullivan found itself with four guards and (center) Becky Clayton on the court."

The next game was a win against an opponent from Louisville, Ky.

After that game, a referee pulled me aside.

"Coach," he said, not knowing better, "your girls were the best-mannered and most polite of any team I had today. They are to be commended."

A loss to Bartonville Limestone in Game 7 brought me back to reality, but the real coach – who was there merely as a fan in the stands – wasn't ready to fire me.

Scott Thomas was, in fact, pleased by the outcome because he wanted, "to keep them from getting complacent."

The Sullivan team went on to win the remainder of its games at Bradley, finishing with a 10-1 record and another tournament championship.

I wrote:

"The team rebounded, not because of the coach, but in spite of the coach."

My conclusion:

"The next time some coach asks, 'Think you can do a better job?' Coach K won't be so quick to respond positively.

"Folks, it ain't as easy as it looks."

From the up-close look I had during the summer, I was convinced that team had the makings of something special. I haven't always been right in my evaluations.

This time I was. Sullivan went 35-0 during the 1990-91 season, won the Class 1A state championship and in the final

USA Today national rankings, came in at No. 14.

The caliber of players on that team can be confirmed by looking at the Illinois Basketball Coaches Association Hall of Fame. Senior standouts Becky Clayton and Amanda Glazebrook were elected to the Hall of Fame as individuals. Junior Sheri Adams – who is now Sullivan's head coach – was enshrined in 2019, also as a player.

Glazebrook's sister, Allyson, would be a freshman on the team the following year when it returned to a state championship game. She, too, was later enshrined in the IBCA state Hall of Fame. Not many small schools (sub-300 enrollments) have produced that much elite talent during the same era.

I've never seen another team at the high school level with the same amount of chemistry, ability and determination as this Sullivan group.

Assortment of awards, credentials and paraphernalia for Fred Kroner.

Fred's Favorites

FAVORITE BOOKS
1. The Five People You Meet in Heaven (Mitch Albom)
2. Travels with Charley (John Steinbeck)
3. Illusions: Adventures of a Reluctant Messiah (Richard Bach)
4. Night (Elie Wiesel)
5. Lord of the Flies (William Golding)
6. On Living (Kerry Egan)

CHAPTER FOURTEEN

My mother died when I was 29 years old.
Naomi Ruth Hillman Kroner was 59.

I never told her I loved her. Not right before she died. Not ever.

Don't think badly of me.

Those weren't words that were spoken in our house. She never said them to me.

My father never spoke them to either of us, at least not in my presence.

We weren't a family of huggers. We didn't show affection easily, if ever.

The best I could hope for was a smile.

One time, when I was in first or second grade, I came home from school and saw my father sitting in his favorite straight-back wooden chair. I did what I had seen cousins do with their dads at family reunions.

I ran to him and jumped in his lap. I landed on the floor. I hadn't missed his lap. He didn't embrace me. Or the idea.

I was scolded. Again.

"You don't do that unless you are invited," he said.

I never made that mistake again.

Naomi Hillman Kroner, wedding day, June 3, 1945.

The 8th of August, 1985 at 8:08 a.m. (If you're keeping track, that's 8/08 at 8:08) wasn't supposed to be my mother's final day on Earth.

She drove herself to what she told me was a routine doctor's appointment the previous Friday. She had been in remission from breast cancer for six months. This was a regularly scheduled checkup.

She called me that night and said the doctor decided he needed to do some tests and that it would be best if she stayed the weekend. She didn't want to alarm me, she said, and there was no reason for me to make a special trip to Mercy Hospital to see her.

I stopped by the following morning anyway. She was in good spirits. Some of the tests wouldn't be completed until Monday, she said. I gave her some reading material.

I had just finished my first non-sports story for The News-Gazette. It was about a young girl from Mahomet whose parents I got acquainted with through a mutual friend. The family shared stories about their daughter, little Megan Lee Fawver, and wondered if I could document her story because so much was happening so fast and they were afraid they would forget important details.

They didn't know how much longer they would have with her. Megan underwent heart surgery when she was 2 ½ days old and had spent much of her life in a hospital room.

I only knew one way to handle this story: to talk with everyone involved. I asked the parents, Tim and Shelby Fawver, to give consent to their team of doctors so I could speak to them about Megan without being told there were privacy issues.

For three months, every moment of my free time was devoted to this project. I wrote two stories. One was the complete, in-depth factual account for the family.

The second was a condensed version that The News-Gazette had already agreed to publish.

The Friday night my mother was admitted to the hospital, I completed the last of the writing and printed out the full version.

I shared that copy with my mother. She joked that she would have plenty of time to read it.

When I returned on Sunday, she told me it was the best story of any I had ever written. The times she didn't like something, she would usually say, "it wasn't one of your best stories."

This one was special, she said.

Here's how it began when published in The News-Gazette on Sunday, Dec 8, 1985:

"Shelby Fawver, thumbing through the local newspaper the other day, was drawn to the obituaries page.

"It wasn't the name which caught her eye, but a portion of the last paragraph, 'Contributions can be made to the Heart Association.'

"The deceased was a 21-month-old girl.

"The story hit home for 24-year-old Shelby Fawver.

"A day doesn't go by when Fawver and her husband, Tim, don't wonder if their daughter's name might appear on the same page.

"Their 11-month-old daughter, Megan Lee, also has a heart defect. She had her first operation when she was just 60 hours old.

"Before the surgery, the family was told, 'She doesn't have a chance.' "

In a sidebar story, published on the same day, I wrote:

"In some respects," said Dr J.J. Shah, "Megan Fawver's future is no more uncertain than anyone's.

"I can't promise her family she will be 50," said Shah, the pediatric cardiologist at Peoria's St. Francis Hospital, "but I can't promise mine that either.

"In most respects, however, Megan's future is very unsettled.

"The type of heart defect that she has is very bad," said Shah. "Almost all of those babies die."

Despite spending almost all of her first five months of life in a hospital, Megan Fawver went on to become a high honors student at Mahomet-Seymour High School. She died in September, 2004, about four months before her 20th birthday. She was a first-semester freshman at Champaign's Parkland College.

During the almost three years I worked at the Bloomington Daily Pantagraph, my mother took out a subscription to keep track of what I was doing.

She would sometimes ask, "Where Is Saunemin?" or "Is San Jose far away?"

She was interested and involved.

And while she never verbalized that she loved me, I felt it. I just hope she recognized my feelings as well.

I asked her one time, prefacing the question with "I think I know the answer to this, but I was wondering…" I asked if my father ever read any of my stories or – because his vision was so poor – had asked her to read any to him.

She told me, "no," but added, "I'm sure he is proud of you."

I returned to the hospital for an after-work visit on Tuesday, Aug. 6, but didn't go the next day. My mother said she hoped she wouldn't be there much longer. Things seemed fine, she said.

My telephone rang on Thursday morning, Aug. 8 at 7:30 a.m. I had just stepped out of the shower.

Naomi R. Kroner, October, 1973, age 47.

The voice on the other end said I should come to the hospital quickly. I was so clueless, I asked what in the world for?

The female voice said something like it shouldn't be discussed over the phone, but that it was important for me to hurry.

I walked into the hospital room at 8:06 a.m. Two minutes later, one of the men in the room said, "she's gone."

I looked at the clock. It said 8:08.

Talk about being unprepared. I was shocked.

When she had said she didn't think she would be there that much longer, I had not prepared myself for that outcome.

Someone asked if I wanted an autopsy to be conducted and I said yes. I needed answers.

When the autopsy results were available, her doctor spoke with me in person rather than by phone.

"The cancer had returned," he said. "It had consumed her lymph nodes."

He asked how much she had complained about being in pain. "Not once," I said.

"There's no way she didn't know," he told me.

So, I asked about the tests that had been taken. What had they shown?

Tests, the doctor wondered.

"We were just trying to make her comfortable," he said.

That was my mom, not wanting to worry or concern others even in her final hours, even in what she must have surely known were her final hours. More than three decades later, I am unable to think about those days without tearing up.

I've often reflected on what life would have been like had the scene in the hospital had been different in just one way. What if my father had passed away when I was 29 and my mother had lived until I was almost 60?

My father had inherited half-interest in a motel in Florida in 1971. By the time of his death in 2014, he had not made one visit to the property. He had a grandson and (at the time of his death) two great grandchildren, but never showed interest or desire in spending time with them either.

Whereas one of the most cherished pictures I have of my

mother is of her holding my son, Devin. It was taken a few months before she died.

I am quite certain if my mother had been granted more years, she would have enjoyed traveling, welcomed time with her grandson and, later, his family.

There are many other things I can now say with confidence that I am right about. As a child, at least in my case, there's a tendency to see the world only the way you want it to be. If the perceptions don't match reality, the blame goes to anyone you are associated with.

In my case, I was sure it was my parents' fault. Why did I have to ride the school bus every single day through my final year of high school? Answer: it was my parents' fault.

Why this? Why that? Why something else? Every question I came up with had the same answer.

Only as I traveled through the path of adulthood did I recognize that the blame was misplaced. It wasn't my collective parents' fault.

In reflection, I remember the many times my mother would tell me, "Your father doesn't want you to do that." I don't remember ever being told, "We don't want you to do that."

As a youngster, I was so busy being mad and disappointed that I didn't see the obvious.

My mother was too kind to speak against my father, but I can see now the decisions were not necessarily ones she would have made or even agreed with. She just wasn't going to rock the boat.

My mother was a kind soul, a gentle soul, a loving soul even if the words were not voiced. I never gave her enough credit for being on my side.

When I was in high school and thought I had written a best-seller, she not only researched the addresses for publishing houses, but paid for all the postage multiple times to send out the manuscript.

Without prompting, she would comment on newspaper stories I had written, saying something that would make it clear she had read it from start to finish.

She even went to an open house at The News-Gazette one Sunday afternoon (which I didn't attend because I was working, covering a baseball doubleheader) to meet our publisher, Mrs. (Marajen) Chinigo and to thank her for hiring me. She didn't quite have the facts right on the hiring process, but the intent blew me away.

The more I think about my mother, the more a line from a Joni Mitchell song comes to mind, "Don't it always seem to go, that you don't know what you've got 'til it's gone?"

*Naomi Hillman,
September, 1942,
senior picture.*

*Naomi Hillman,
undated.*

*Naomi Kroner and
Devin Kroner, January,
1985. On Naomi's 59th
birthday. Devin was
22-months old.*

CHAPTER FIFTEEN

Through the years, I have worked with three different people named Bob Jones and two named John Smith. As far as I know, none of the Joneses or Smiths were related.

As much as I enjoyed all of those individuals, there was something special to me to not have to share a last name with anyone outside of some relatives.

And then one day, one of the weirdest things that ever happened while I was on the job took place at quaint Danville Stadium, which is one of my favorite places to watch a baseball game.

The exact date escapes me, but it was around 2010 or 2011 after the Danville Dans opened their summer collegiate league season in early June.

I took my seat in the press box and waited for the public address announcer to arrive.

There were several individuals who alternated and I never knew in advance which one to expect.

On this particular night, it was a person I had not previously met.

He introduced himself as Tuck Miller.

I told him I was Fred Kroner.

He looked at me like he had seen a ghost.

"What did you say your name was," he asked.

"Fred Kroner," I repeated.

He wanted to know how it was spelled and if I had ever been to California or had relatives there.

I answered his questions and inquired why he was asking.

Miller proceeded to tell me that he had lived in California and worked on the railroad. The name of his boss was Fred Kroner.

Same spelling.

He then pulled out his cell phone and made a call.

I heard him ask for Fred. He then said, "there's someone here you need to talk to."

I got on the phone and said, "Hi. This is Fred Kroner."

The voice on the other end said, "Hi. I am Fred Kroner."

We chatted for a few minutes and then I had to turn my attention to the ball game.

I've never had an experience like that.

As far as I know, we're not related. But then again, we must be.

Fred Kroner watches the action at Mary Miller Gymnasium, at Danville Area Community College, during a session of the NJCAA men's Division II basketball tournament.

Weird is the best description of that night.

That brief conversation brought flashbacks to a March night, in 1994.

I was leaving Mary Miller Gymnasium, on the Danville Area Community College campus, after the final session in the NJCAA men's basketball tournament (the first year the event was held in Danville).

What should I see as I exited at about 10 p.m. but my picture? Larger than life, my face was plastered on the

Placards used on boxes where newspapers were sold. The graphics are mini versions of what were on buses.

side of a city bus with the words, "Vermilion County Sports Authority."

Good thing I was by myself because I was speechless. No one from the newspaper had even mentioned to me that they were starting this particular advertising campaign.

It's unexplainably weird to see an image of yourself where your face alone is so enlarged it covers about 3 feet in depth.

The advertising folks at The News-Gazette had to tell me a few years later when they produced a follow-up campaign.

This time I was required to go to the Vermilion County Public Safety Building and have a 'mugshot' taken where the officers book individuals who have been arrested.

This time, the ad campaign was "Vermilion County's Most Wanted," which I took to mean the person newspaper readers most wanted to read. My face was on the poster, but behind some bars.

It struck me as odd that not once have I been on the inside of a Danville city bus, but for months in two different years I was "on" the outside of the bus.

This story actually has a third part.

A friend sent me a sports story he thought I might be interested in. The part I found most fascinating was the byline.

It was written by Steve Kroner, of the San Francisco Chronicle.

I was not aware of any relatives on the West Coast, but the knowledge of my family tree only goes back about four generations.

In 2019, I emailed Steve Kroner to see if he might have knowledge of a mutual relative from way back.

He didn't, but offered a story somewhat similar to mine with my random meeting with Tuck Miller. His story even took place at a baseball game.

"A few years ago, I was covering a Giants' game," Steve Kroner wrote. "A man came to the press box to say 'Hi.'

"He was another Kroner who lived somewhere in northern California. I sadly forgot his first name – I think he went by the nickname Lefty – but it was fun talking to him."

It was nice to hear from Steve Kroner, who has been in the sports-journalism industry since 1981, when he graduated from Cal, but it was also a little sad, too.

It just means that I'm less unique than I thought. The good news is that the Kroner byline continues and now encompasses parts of two centuries, and that has to be a good thing.

Write on.

Attention: Retail House
Ad Number: SP16069   Status: Complete
Ad Description:·
Size: 3 x 5' · Actual Size: 5.792" x 5'
Sales Rep: Glenda Hutchinson
Sales Assistant: None
Client Approval: OK_____ Corrections_____ Signature _____
Start Date: End Date: -
Insertion Date   Publication

Current Date: Thu, Aug 21, 2008 - 10:47 AM
Proofs Created:0
        Color:·
Last User: Joan Mills
Phone: 217-351-5282
Fax: 217-351-5291
        Total Insertions: 0
                Class Code

Sample ad in The News-Gazette, August 2008.

Meet Fred Kroner,
prep football's biggest fan

You think you love football!

News-Gazette sports reporter Fred Kroner lives and breathes it and he's traveling to a high school near you. You can "catch" Fred at these games:

Let the games begin. **The News-Gazette**

CHAPTER SIXTEEN

How do you measure the success of a person's career? In my view, there's not one unified set of standards. It varies by profession.

For educators, criteria can certainly be lives impacted. Some teachers – such as my high school journalism teacher, Linda Cooper – have a profound affect and can't be forgotten, or thanked enough.

A few years after I was hired at The News-Gazette, and with the help of an acquaintance from Mahomet, I was able to track down Linda Cooper in Ohio. I called her and thanked her for the guidance and encouragement she provided that wound up leading to my career choice.

She appreciated hearing from me and mentioned she was only in Mahomet for a short period of time. For me, it was long enough to make a difference in at least one young person's life.

For journalists, the category of lives impacted is not really applicable like it is for educators. I am sure there are some people we have impacted due to providing them with a few extra clippings for their scrapbooks. But it's really more nebulous. You have to look beyond the obvious.

In 2006, I interviewed some high school athletes who helped to put things in perspective.

Merry Lanker graduated from Monticello High School in 2004. She shared these thoughts:

"Being interviewed a few times was thrilling," Lanker said. "I always appreciated it because Monticello High School usually laminated and posted the clipping to our lockers at school for everyone to see.

"It was a huge honor to be interviewed. Honestly, I think that the possibility of being interviewed might have somehow contributed to a few of my best races, specifically the Tuscola and St. Joe road races my senior year."

Kyle Leeman was a 2005 Georgetown-Ridge Farm High School graduate. He said talking with reporters and having newspaper clippings to reflect on were a highlight.

"I am glad I played in an area in which the local newspapers cared about prep sports," Leeman said. "I believe the media helps make high school athletics more fun.

"Just having your name in the paper was something that was always special. I tried to include teammates every time, but sometimes that was hard to do."

Perhaps journalists have changed lives by providing information that people did not realize, or presented it in a way they had not considered, prompting them to alter decisions they were pondering. We'd like to think and hope we're making a difference in more than a few isolated instances, but there is usually not empirical data to show it.

Of course, there are the rare exceptions.

Cheyenne Hedrington comes to my mind. By featuring her in a story I wrote on Saturday, April 21, 2012, when she was a high school senior, it set the wheels in motion to give her an assist at a time when it was most needed.

Hedrington was a basketball player who started her prep career at Champaign Centennial and wound up graduating from Champaign Central the spring of 2012. The story focused more on her background than her exploits as a player, which were considerable. She was a team captain as both a junior and as a senior.

During her eighth-grade year, after her parents divorced, Hedrington and her mother, Rhonda Overcast, were officially homeless when their house was foreclosed within a year. They spent time with assorted relatives before moving on, Overcast said, because "we were interrupting someone else's life." This was a pattern they followed for three years.

I wrote: "Some stories you read or hear about are heart-wrenching sagas about families torn apart by a divorce, then losing their home to foreclosure with a single mother on disability left behind to raise a teenage daughter.

"The perception is these stories come from afar, not in the community or the neighborhood where we live.

"The reality is these incidents occur anywhere and everywhere. Sometimes, varsity athletes whose careers have been documented in the newspaper for years are individuals who have spent a majority of their time in high school without a permanent place to call home.

"The 'before' and 'after' pictures of Cheyenne Hedrington would paint a start contrast."

Basketball was a means for Hedrington to get a college education. She had a scholarship to John Wood College, in Quincy, Ill., that would start in the fall of 2012.

"When I'd step on the court and play, it seemed like nothing else in the world mattered," Hedrington told me. "It made me push harder. I'd take my anger out on my opponents."

Hedrington was anxious to get a jump-start on both her college education and getting familiar with her new teammates and wanted to enroll in summer school. The story mentioned that her scholarship wasn't available until fall and she was going to get a weekend job to pay for summer tuition.

It was said in a matter-of-fact manner, not with the intention of solicitation. And yet, before the story had been in print for 24 hours, two anonymous sources contacted me at the office wondering how they could make a donation.

The end result: Soon her summer tuition and fees were covered. The donors never came forward to be identified. They didn't want any publicity or recognition.

Hedrington eventually earned a bachelor's degree from Grand Canyon College in Arizona, the first person from her family with a college diploma. She followed it up by earning a master's degree and, as of this writing, is working on her doctorate. She has also been playing basketball overseas.

Her goals were well-established long before she set foot on a college campus.

"I'll make something of myself and be there to help my family," Hedrington said.

For me, those are the feel-good stories I cherish as much as covering an individual or a team that wins a state championship. I may never see Cheyenne Hedrington again, but I will certainly never forget her.

Journalists are sometimes evaluated for the awards they win. That is bogus recognition; not that I want to return any of the honors I have received.

I recognize how subjective these awards are, having both served as a judge for writing contests and having submitted entries to various state and national contests.

Depending on the category, decisions are often made by one person. Occasionally, it's a two-person process with the first one culling down the myriad entries to a manageable number, such as 10 or 15 and then a second individual deciding which three or four will get honored.

When looking at three-plus decades of making submissions, here's what I see: stories that are about subjects you don't typically hear much about tend to fare better at contest time. When I had topics such as the number of black athletes participating in volleyball, high school athletes admitting to drug use, and the climate for gay and lesbian high school coaches, those stories fared better as entries than ones about an athlete who spent his summer in Marine Boot Camp and then returned to high school for his senior season.

Over the years, some of the articles that were (in my opinion!) the best-written and most creative I had done, were overlooked at contest time while others which required considerably less effort and I wasn't as pleased with, were honored.

Don't get me wrong. Many deserving writers have gotten the recognition they were due. I look back on the national honors bestowed upon Rick Reilly and all I can think is, "There probably should have been more."

Personally, more meaningful is recognition that comes as the result of a body of work. The Illinois Wrestling Coaches and Officials Association selected me as Newsman of the Year four times. It wasn't an award I applied for, but one that came about based on my coverage of the sport throughout the regular season and the state tournament series.

It was the same when the Illinois Softball Coaches Association made a similar presentation and when the Illinois Basketball Coaches Association honored me with induction into their Hall of Fame.

The most humbling was being chosen by my peers as Sportswriter of the Year for the state of Illinois in 2001. There is one selection a year (plus one for sports broadcasters, too) and dozens of newspapers with deserving candidates.

Being presented the award at the National Sportswriters and Sportscasters Association annual banquet, in Salisbury, N.C., by Rick Reilly was even more special.

In one of those ironic twists, the day we were leaving and hailed a cab for the airport, as we opened the car door, a voice said, "is there room for one more?"

Fred Kroner's 2001 plaque for recognition as the Sportswriter of the Year for Illinois from the National Sportscasters and Sportswriters Association.

It was Rick Reilly. We were happy to make room for him. The ride to the airport was too short; far too short.

There is a point – and it's not to brag – in mentioning the assortment of awards and honors.

For everything I have done, there is one thing I can't do. However, I don't think I am alone.

It's impossible to tell someone how to write a good story. You have to see it, visualize it, feel it.

The best I can do is offer a few tips and pointers to get someone started.

This may sound silly, but I approach every feature story

as if I were writing about a family member. I want it to be special and if that means devoting extra time to research or interviewing an extra source or two, so be it. Thoroughness and depth are qualities I find lacking in many newspaper articles I read.

The quality of a story is much more important than how quickly it is finished. I never submit a story without re-reading and proofreading it at least twice. I'm tweaking words and phrases constantly.

It is my opinion that every story can be improved if the writer is willing to look for the ways, and then make the extra effort. Sometimes this isn't practical because there are deadlines to meet and other stories to write.

I'm guessing that at least three-fourths of the game stories I've written on tight deadlines were re-playing in my mind as I drove home when I suddenly thought of better ways to say things, or points that I had overlooked magically became clear. At that time, of course, it was too late. The story was in print and no changes or updates were possible.

As I consider which approach or angle to take with a story, I keep in mind that I'm not going to write something that I wouldn't want to read. I'm always looking for insight and perspective, something that goes beyond the game or event I just covered.

In decades past, football game stories were written in a chronological manner, starting with the first quarter and concluding with the fourth quarter, even if the game-winning touchdown was scored in the final 10 seconds. I know this from scanning reels and reels of microfilm, something I routinely did for decades to find information or to confirm facts.

I advocated for a different style. People don't truly care for a play-by-play recap of any sporting event. They want to know what the outcome means, they want to know what the coach was thinking when a particular play was called, what the athlete was thinking when the play broke down and he had to create something on the spur of the moment.

People want emotions, whether it's joy or agony. They want more than what they can get by watching the game, whether they view it in person or on television. They want to know what a particular game or outcomes means, why a specific individual was the focus of the story.

They want to be taken inside the team, inside the minds of the players or coaches and, especially, to learn something they didn't already know.

There were plenty of people who didn't like this approach when The News-Gazette first began turning game stories into feature opportunities in the 1990s. It's natural to not embrace change immediately, especially when it is drastic.

Perhaps I went overboard at times, covering a game and getting so caught up in the story I was telling that I didn't get the final score mentioned until the 10th or 12th paragraph. One of our former editors insisted on the score being included no lower than the third paragraph and if it wasn't there, the story would be rewritten to get it there.

I've spent hours and hours, over the entire course of my career, studying microfilm. I'm certain that Tom Kacich and myself were the two most frequent microfilm users during my 34 ½ years with The News-Gazette. Kacich was an editorial writer and had a penchant for research.

You can learn so much, studying the history and patterns of how stories were handled previously as well as the background of particular schools or events. I love the process, the hunt for how something was way back when. I love to compare and contrast.

In the final three years that Tom Stewart was the Champaign Central football head coach, I had an extra reason to regularly check microfilm.

During our weekly visits, Stewart would routinely talk about games from the past, sometimes more than a quarter of a century earlier. He would remember specifics, such as how far a player ran for a touchdown, the weather conditions and other factoids like the number of passes his team attempted, that were impressive to a person who can't always remember to pick up a prescription the same day it is phoned in.

I never told Stewart I was doing this, but I would make notes about the games and details he mentioned and then track down the game story on microfilm. I think the closest I ever came to finding an error was when he said a certain TD run was 68 yards and the game story listed it as 67 yards.

There was something else unique about Stewart, at least in his waning years as a head coach. He created three-platoon football. He had an offensive unit, a defensive unit and also a special teams unit, which meant each game, 33 different squad members could consider themselves as starters. It was no wonder the roster size from freshmen through seniors was above 130.

When it comes to writing a story, there are certain basics that are non-negotiable. Every fact must be accurate. Quotes must be attributed. Keep in mind that columns – or opinion pieces – are different from straight news stories and the two types can't be mixed.

Opinions should never be interjected into a hard news story.

I've found it amazing how many different approaches writers covering the same national event take. It's not just the words that are different, it's the entire viewpoint.

Writing is not at all like mathematics. When you add three to five, there is only one correct answer, and we can explain to others how to determine that answer.

Writing is freelance. There is not a right or wrong way to

compose a story. Some ways are better or more interesting than others just like some runners are naturally faster than others.

Give me a stack of 25 stories and I can pick the five best. Give that same stack to someone else and it's possible five different stories will be selected.

That doesn't mean one person is right and the other is wrong. It means there are a multitude of effective ways to tell a story.

I don't know how I do it, but some way I do.

As for the success of my career, I'd prefer to let others be the judge. All I know is that it was an adventurous ride.

Fred's Favorites

FAVORITE TELEVISION SHOWS

1. Blue Bloods
2. Columbo
3. Diagnosis: Murder
4. Murder She Wrote
5. Mork and Mindy
6. Walker, Texas Ranger

CHAPTER SEVENTEEN

In theory, the best is saved for last, or at least near the end. Depending on your perspective, that is what I have done as I reflected on my life's history and the good days, bad days, highlights and lowlights.

I'm lucky to be here today.

I should have realized that 41 years ago, but my one-track mind – making deadline – prevented it.

It was Sept. 15, 1978, my first year of covering high school football at the Bloomington Daily Pantagraph.

The sports department's structure was different than all other newspapers with which I have been associated. Rather than have people who were strictly writers and others who were strictly bound to office duties, there was a rotation system.

I might cover Friday night football two weeks in a row and spend the following two Fridays working in the office. It was hard for me to get into a groove and produce consistently good copy because I work best when I have repeated opportunities day after day.

On this particular Friday, I was assigned a football game in Chenoa, north and a bit east of Bloomington.

The Pantagraph had a fleet of company cars, but the night-time writers had to share them with the day-time advertising reps. Sometimes the advertising reps were back by the time we needed to leave for a game, and sometimes they weren't. Our own cars got a workout more often than not.

I was able to get a company vehicle that night, the second Friday of the high school football season. Chenoa was playing Forrest-Strawn-Wing (a high school with one of my favorite mascots, the Eskimos).

The game itself was pretty uneventful and non-descript, with Chenoa winning 34-0.

However, as the game continued and the evening grew later, a thick fog started settling in. I was concerned about merging onto Interstate 55 heading south for fear I might collide with another car. The fog was really that dense.

My entrance to the interstate was successful. In fact, I didn't see any cars or trucks in front or behind me, which is pretty odd for 9:30 on a Friday night.

Without warning, I suddenly saw a single red tail light directly in front of me, on the right side. At first, I thought it was a car that had pulled off to the side of the road. Then, I realized it was a semi that had its left rear taillight out.

I reacted on impulse, swerved to my left, silently praying that no one was passing me at that moment.

I am certain my reaction would have been perfect had I been in my personal vehicle. I was in an unfamiliar company car, with power steering. I could probably count the number of times on one hand that I had driven a car with power steering prior to that day.

I dramatically overcorrected and instead of continuing to go forward on the highway, the car flipped over three times. Each time it crashed to the ground, the full force of the impact came on the passenger side.

After the third flip, the car wobbled and then remained perched on its top. The driver's window was completely shattered. I grabbed my clipboard, crawled out and tried to figure out what to do next.

I had no injuries except for a small cut on my forehead.

This was 1978, pre-cell phones. It didn't seem safe to stand by the road and hitchhike. No one would possibly see me.

Before I could formulate a plan, I was aware of red and blue flashing lights and a voice saying, "is everyone all right?"

The state police officer said he saw the headlights in the median (the car, which I had been driving south, wound up facing north). I explained what happened, told him I was alone and asked if there was any way he could get me back to Bloomington.

He asked which hospital I wanted to go to and I said, neither. I wanted him to drop me off at The Pantagraph.

He asked a few more questions, I think to make sure I was truly coherent and then agreed to let me ride with him to town. He first called a towing company to pick up the car. Would that even happen now, or would the officer be required to stay on the scene until the tow truck had arrived? We left right after the call was made.

That was my first – and only – time riding in a police car.

I was thankful for the lift and, as I recall, was at the office only about 15 minutes later than if I had driven myself without the interruption.

After passing security at The Pantagraph, I went directly to the restroom because I wasn't really sure how disheveled I looked. I found a slight tear in the knee of my jeans, but otherwise I saw no obvious damage. I washed off the scrape on my face.

Then I proceeded to write my story before I mentioned anything about the accident to my co-workers.

After researching the history of the series in advance, the storyline was obvious.

My article began, "The results of recent Forrest-Strawn-

Wing/Chenoa football games have been very predictable
– the team that scores first wins – as the last nine games have
been shutouts.

"That tradition was continued Friday night as Chenoa
tallied at least once in every quarter to blank the Eskimos,
34-0."

When the officer dropped me off at The Pantagraph office,
he told me where the vehicle would be towed, to a location
on West Market St. One of my colleagues offered me a ride
home after our shifts ended, but first we drove by the lot
where the car was stowed.

Seeing the vehicle under the street lights made me realize
that I wasn't alone. I had an angel riding with me. It was
amazing to think that anyone had survived as badly as
the car was mangled on the right side. And yet, I not only
survived, but also didn't even need any treatment at a
hospital.

I was 22 years old and thankful to be given a second
chance at life. I haven't taken a day for granted since then,
and every day am thankful for what I have been given.

In my remaining time with the company, I still occasionally
drove Pantagraph cars, but the biggest change I made was to
trade my own vehicle for one with power steering, so I could
get accustomed to the feel of the steering wheel.

Is it any surprise that to this day I would rather stay home
than drive in fog?

CHAPTER EIGHTEEN

I always knew I'd write a book. More accurately, I always knew I would *like* to write a book.

I actually accomplished the goal at a young age.

I sort of got a start as an 18-year-old sophomore in college when I self-published a book of original poetry in September, 1974. I wanted the title to represent the greatest contrasts I could think of, so I came up with "Asphalt Celery." I even wrote a poem to go with the title.

A buddy from high school, my biology lab partner Mark Page, did the artwork. I'm pretty sure he never got paid.

I went to a company on Green Street, Andromeda, that offered printing services and self-published a rudimentary paperback. Five hundred copies of the 32-page typewritten booklet were printed and distributed at various stores throughout the UI campus as well as a drug store in Mahomet.

Stores were willing to display the books in a "local authors" section. None of the stores bought the books from me, but were willing to sell them (for $4 apiece) on a commission basis and give me half of the proceeds. I cashed in to the tune of $6. I never got the unsold books back, however.

They were the best poems I had written at that age, but as I look back decades later, they wouldn't make a list of my top 250.

After that experience, it was more than a quarter of a century before I even thought about writing another book.

This time, another childhood friend got everything orchestrated. Walter Pierce was working at Sports Publishing, on Neil Street, in Champaign. The company had already printed a dozen or so sports books, targeted for a young audience of fifth- or sixth-graders.

I had a long association with Pierce. I would regularly hang out at his house on days of our high school basketball games. If I rode the school bus home immediately after school, I had no way to get back to town in time for the basketball bus departure. And, after being at school all day, I wasn't anxious to spend another 90 minutes to two hours hanging out in the building.

His mom had plenty of mouths to feed, but didn't seem to mind when I showed up multiple times a month for a late-afternoon snack during the winter.

Subjects of the early Sports Publishing books included popular professional athletes such as Ken Griffey Jr., Peyton Manning, Dale Earnhardt Jr., Jim Thome, Ken Norton, Mark McGwire and others. Most were priced at $9.95.

"They didn't sell very well," Pierce said.

His suggestion was to focus a book on someone well-known in the Champaign-Urbana community, a local celebrity-type approach. Brian Cardinal seemed to be the ideal candidate.

Cardinal was raised just south of Champaign, in Tolono, Ill. He was a star basketball player at Unity High School and went on to become a four-year starter in college at Purdue University, scoring nearly 1,600 points for the Boilermakers.

In 2000, Cardinal was a second-round draft choice by the Detroit Pistons. He had completed a transformation from a small-school prep star at a school of about 400 students to the National Basketball Association.

As Cardinal completed his rookie season in the NBA, the book on his life to that point was published. I got 112 pages out of it, and that included at least 10 pages of pictures. We priced it at $6.95.

It was called "Brian Cardinal, Citizen Pain," a tribute to a nickname he had earned during this collegiate career with the Purdue University Boilermakers.

A total of 5,000 books were printed in September, 2001, and Pierce said, "we made money on that book."

Each book I've written had a unique set of challenges. With the Cardinal book, one difficulty was having access to him in person for just part of one afternoon, totaling about 90 minutes.

The other challenge was reaching out to a plethora of people whom I had no connection with and thus they weren't always prompt in returning calls. With persistence, I tracked down Cardinal's college coach, Gene Keady, as well as his first NBA coach, George Irvine.

My next book literally fell into my lap. Jim Sheppard was the long-time public address announcer for UI football and men's basketball games.

My bosses at The News-Gazette learned that he was not going to be retained for the following year and wanted me to write his life's history.

It was called, "Are You Ready?" and subtitled, "Jim Sheppard – a career announcing Illinois football and basketball." It had 178 pages and sold for $12.95 when released in 2007.

I had about three months to do all the interviews and writing. That was three months in addition to working my regular job.

I never took a leave of absence to work on any of the books.

I devoted time to the project in the early-morning or late-night hours after doing my "day job." That's why there were several years between books.

One benefit with the Sheppard project was that he was working in the advertising department at The Gazette at the time, so I had virtually unlimited access to him. We talked or exchanged notes almost every day of the work week.

I had hardly turned in the finished version when I decided to suggest an idea for Book No. 3. I scheduled a meeting in publisher John Foreman's office and explained how the amateur Eastern Illinois Baseball League was closing in on its 75th year of existence.

I wanted to write a complete history of the storied E.I. League.

He consented and said the newspaper would stand behind the project. This was a significant commitment as I learned with the Sheppard book.

Since The News-Gazette was publishing the books, they handled other key components like arranging for newspaper ads, setting up book signing sessions and distribution to area bookstores.

Years later, I would discover how truly valuable it was to have that support.

The E.I. book was a labor of love. For years, I had been researching the league, not with the idea of putting it into book form, but to try and gather and preserve the history and the iconic moments.

Though I had a good start, it took two more years of work to reach the point where I was confident that I had all of the information that was available and could start organizing and writing.

I knew about the league because I was able to succeed E.W. Hesse as The News-Gazette sportswriter who covered the weekly summer games. Starting in 1984, I didn't miss a week of games through the 1993 season, unless all sites were rained out.

That association had enabled me to meet many of the people I wanted to feature in the book. It was a delight to reach them again, capture memories and include their stories in the book.

By the time I retired from The Gazette, in August, 2015, I was no longer covering the E.I. on a regular basis, but had been chosen as the league's President, a position I also left in 2015.

Of all the books I wrote, the E.I. book, entitled "Catching Up," was my favorite. It was also my first hard-cover book, which made it extra special. It was published in 2010 and was priced at $19.95 for the 170-page volume.

It was subtitled, "The official history of the Eastern Illinois Baseball League."

Next up was another historical profile, on the UI Assembly Hall. The Gazette wanted to have it completed prior to the 50th anniversary of the building's opening (March 2, 1963) and we made the deadline. Barely.

We called it, "A Saucer Coming To Rest," and subtitled it, "A half century of the Assembly Hall."

Copies of the 120-page book (priced at $29.95) were delivered on the Friday before the 2013 UI home finale, which was the next day. We set up a booth outside one of the first-floor entrances at the Assembly Hall, but only had modest sales. People didn't have much advance notice and I think most didn't want to haul a book around throughout the game.

This book – my first to feature color pictures – was the hardest to pull off because the key people involved in the construction and design of the building – such as architect Max Abramovitz – were deceased.

Buildings don't talk, so to tell the story properly, I had to rely on patrons and performers to discuss the importance and prominence of the iconic building. Old newspaper clippings were a huge help, too.

Most frustrating for me: Six weeks after the book was released, the UI called a press conference to detail the renaming of the building as the State Farm Center, an agreement that will last for 30 years, or until 2043.

Timing is everything. If that announcement had been made three months sooner, it would have provided a wonderful conclusion to the book while encompassing the entire lifespan that it was known as the Assembly Hall.

The Assembly Hall book was the final one I wrote that was coordinated through The News-Gazette.

In February of 2016, I self-published what I consider the best-written and most informative of the first six books I've authored. It chronicled the unbeaten season of Parkland College's 2015 national championship volleyball team.

It was entitled "Parkland Perfection," and subtitled, "Be together, not the same." It was 134 pages, not including a special 26-page section of color pictures. It was paperback and sold for $19.95.

I expected it to have wide appeal because of the focus on the team's various players and coaches as opposed to merely recapping the matches. There were fascinating stories, such as how a player from Australia became a Parkland Cobra, how a player from Idaho who had never been scouted by the coaches wound up on campus as well as the relationship of the two male coaches, who became parents of twins shortly after the season ended.

However, I was on my own for everything from editing to marketing, from advertising to distribution. Since I had to pay all of the costs of publishing and layout up front, it left little available for advertising. As a result, I have more of these books in storage than all of my others combined.

This autobiography becomes the seventh and – I anticipate – the final book I will write.

However, I have learned to never say 'never.'

CHAPTER NINETEEN

I only know one way to do things. That is, to the best of my abilities without cutting any corners.

My concern was never the number of hours in my work week, but what needed to be done. It's a work ethic I learned on the farm when it was imperative to take advantage of favorable weather conditions as they presented themselves.

An example from my newspaper career comes to mind.

My long-time News-Gazette colleague, Jean McDonald, was a champion for prep sports and – in particular – a balance and equality for girls' sports, which made their debut in many Illinois high schools in the mid-1970s.

The News-Gazette had implemented All-State teams in football and boys' basketball decades earlier and they were a staple of the paper. The football team was always published on Thanksgiving Day, and still is.

McDonald organized All-State teams for girls' basketball and volleyball. She and I were like-minded in wanting to make as certain as possible that no deserving candidate was ever overlooked. She sent mailings to every high school in the state which offered either volleyball (for a team chosen in the late fall) or girls' basketball (for teams chosen in the late winter) requesting nominations.

Of course, there was never 100 percent response, but it was a great starting point. The form that we asked coaches to fill out also included a spot for them to mention 10 players from opposing schools who had impressed them throughout the season.

Every coach is going to think their player is a bonafide prospect, but if 20 opposing coaches mentioned the same player, that means more than if the athlete is recognized by just one or two opposing coaches.

As McDonald transitioned from her status as a sportswriter to the editor position, she had less time to devote to selecting these honor teams. Joe Millas handled the selections for a few years and then I took over in 1990 and was in charge of the All-State project for the girls' teams for 25 years.

I continued the mailings to coaches for years, finally

News-Gazette volleyball Player of the Year Amber McKean in a classroom at Cissna Park in November, 2003. Sportswriter Fred Kroner (far left) shadowed her for an entire school day

switching to email forms a few years before I retired.

Email made the initial contact easier, but I continued with a longstanding tradition after the teams were picked. I made sure every first-teamer (not only on All-State teams, but also on our All-Area teams) received a personal letter which I wrote, along with a certificate as well as a copy of the All-State (or All-Area) edition.

***

It was time-consuming, but something I considered a good-will project to show others throughout the state how seriously we took these teams and that it truly was an honor to be recognized. It was also something tangible that the young athlete could possess as a keepsake. Most of this work was done on my own time since my bosses didn't consider it a priority.

Most years, I enlisted some of our stellar part-timers to help address envelopes. Nathan Kurtz, Larry Drake, Troy Gentle and Bob Jones were four of the individuals I recruited the most and they were responsive, even though it meant less time to do the other jobs they were hired to do.

During my tenure, I took pride in having a photo of every individual chosen to the first All-State teams in both volleyball and girls' basketball. I considered it important and – more than once – coaches had to send a picture in overnight mail because they had neglected to submit one in a timely manner when requested a month earlier.

To me, those touches are ones which add to the overall product and to show that we – as a newspaper – truly cared.

Selecting the All-Area teams had an additional component which I took seriously. The News-Gazette circulation area, at one time, included about 50 high schools. Consolidations and co-op arrangements had reduced that number to around

40 high schools by my departure.

I made sure to see all schools play that had a viable candidate, which was usually at least 35 of the schools. When combined with other items on my checklist, it was an important consideration. You can tell a lot even before the games start by watching how players warm up. You can also see how they respond when facing a high-caliber opponent.

That's why statistical data was merely one of many factors that led to the final selection. What did the player do for her team? Was she well-rounded and able to contribute in multiple ways? Was she a good teammate who made sure to involve others?

At first, it was a daunting task, but as the years progressed, it became a natural part of what I did and I was as comfortable making the picks as I was covering a ball game.

I was never successful in getting softball added to the list of sports where we selected All-State squads. In part, that was due to the need to have a matching All-State team for baseball and as newspaper staff sizes were shrinking, there wasn't the time or the personnel to make this a reality.

Five years after I officially retired, I still feel bad that the athletes in these spring sports could not receive All-State accolades from the newspaper.

It was especially pleasing, though, to be involved on the ground level when The News-Gazette rolled out All-Area teams for what some consider the minor sports, such as wrestling, cross-country, golf, swimming, tennis and track and field. Eventually, we created a listing for Coach of the Year in every sport as well.

Jim Rossow gets the credit for this idea and, after he announced plans to implement these additional All-Area teams, he told me, "Make it happen."

These are ways to get people looking at the newspaper who

might not have read it closely before. The hope is they will like what they see and want to become a regular subscriber or advertiser.

Fred's Favorites

FAVORITE SITES TO COVER EVENTS

1. Milford's blue-carpeted gymnasium
2. LaSalette's throwback gymnasium
3. Harper Park, rural Royal
4. Chrisman Cowchip Cross-Country Course
5. Jacksonville's bowl
6. Huff Gymnasium

The News-Gazette

March 1, 1990

Courtney:

On behalf of The News-Gazette, let me congratulate you on your selection to our all-area basketball team as well as to our All-State basketball team.

Both honors were well deserved.

I certainly enjoyed watching you and Shiloh play when I had the opportunity this season. I appreciate your time and consideration when I had the chance to talk with you.

I'm looking forward to getting the chance to seeing you play at Illinois State ... if not this summer in PSG.

Best wishes and if there's anything else I can do for you, please don't hesitate to ask.

FRED KRONER

News-Gazette Sportswriter

Marajen Stevick Chinigo
Publisher & Chairman of the Board

John C. Hirschfeld
President & Chief Executive Officer

15 Main Street, P.O. Box 677, Champaign, IL 61824-0677 ☎ 217-351-5252

All-State letter to Courtney Porter, March 1990.

CHAPTER TWENTY

I'm an only child who often writes letters or emails to Brother Ed. I usually get responses addressed to Brother Fred.

Ed Glennon is a Bement native and no relation, at least as far as we know.

Here's how the story got started.

Glennon worked his way through the University of Illinois in the 1980s and was a part-time sportswriter at The News-Gazette. He liked to shadow me on some of my game-night assignments.

Ed Glennon and Fred Kroner, June, 2015.

On Feb. 21, 1984, we went to a Rantoul boys' basketball game at Danville Schlarman High School. We went to the viewing spot I preferred, just behind the scorer's table (in case I missed something, I could get an immediate answer).

Rantoul had three high school girls serving as stat-keepers, Paula Adametz (now Hays), Jill Flessner (now Jones) and Kathy Ihnen (now Lutes). They looked at us intently as we seated ourselves on the bleachers.

Finally, one of them spoke. "Are you guys brothers?"

We have the same basic build and were each wearing glasses. I suppose there was some resemblance.

Ed immediately responded, 'This is my brother, Fred,' and I followed up and said that he was my brother Ed.

I'm not sure the girls really believed us, but for the next 35 years, that is how Ed and I have referred to each other.

I think, in fact, if I had been blessed with a brother, I would want it to be someone just like Ed, who switched from an illustrious sportswriting career to one as a high school English teacher at Belvidere North.

The story doesn't end there, however.

In 2014 I was covering a swim meet at Centennial High School when a woman approached me on the deck.

"I don't know if you remember me…" she started.

Admittedly, I couldn't place the face. Then, she told me her name.

It was the former Paula Adametz.

Of course, I remembered her, Jill and Kathy. Without them, I might never have had a "brother."

Glennon was with me for several memorable highlights.

I once wrote a column supporting a tactic favored by Champaign Central boys' basketball coach Lee Cabutti. The Hall-of-Famer liked to play slow-down ball and keep games close, hoping for a spurt in the game's final minute to pull out a win against an opponent that – on paper – appeared vastly superior.

My column discussed the merits of this approach. Players had to be disciplined and adept at handling the ball. They had to be able to play under pressure because every possession becomes vitally critical when they are reduced in number.

At several Central basketball games which I covered that season, I kept track of how many passes the team made after crossing halfcourt before attempting a shot. It wasn't unusual to see more than 150 passes prior to a shot being launched.

The January night in 1984 that Glennon accompanied me to Combes Gym – and, incidentally, the court itself is now named in Cabutti's honor – there was a vociferous Central student cheering section just behind the team bench on the west side of the gymnasium.

It didn't take long before they engaged in a cheer they had obviously prepared and practiced in advance.

"One. Two. Three. Four. What the hell we stalling for? Hey Fred."

The part I liked best? It showed that at least some of these teen-agers had been reading the newspaper.

I found it amusing that they directed the end of the chant to me, as opposed to the head coach, who clearly makes the decisions on such strategies.

Cabutti could handle the criticism. "Going into the last quarter, we had a chance to win," he said, in defense of his ball-control philosophy. "Nobody ever ran away from us."

There's a first time for everything and in this particular case, a last time as well. I've never had another cheer which featured me.

Word spread fast, too, in an era that preceded Facebook, Twitter, Instagram and Snapchat. When I arrived back at the office that night, the newsroom was abuzz about the cheer which was directed to me.

Cabutti was a sportswriter's dream. He was a coach who wasn't afraid to speak his mind or who would say something and follow it with the phrase, "That's off the record."

One vintage comment from Cabutti was spoken in March, 2015, when he and his wife, JoAnne, were presented keys to the City of Champaign.

Said Cabutti: "People must think I have one foot in the grave and the other on a banana peel."

I made it a point to arrive at Central basketball games I was covering prior to the start of the junior varsity contest.

From left, John Spezia, Lee Cabutti and Fred Kroner.

Cabutti and I would sit in the stands and chit-chat about various things. I'll always remember him sharing that his first year in teaching he coached three sports at Herrin, Ill. His salary for the 1951-52 school year, including the coaching increments, was $3,100.

It was my pleasure to cover a number of his games in his final season as the Central head coach, 1984-85. He announced in the preseason it would be his final year on the sidelines.

Practically every out-of-town trip resulted in a presentation to Cabutti. At Stephen Decatur, coach Rease Binger gave him a rocking chair.

Cabutti's son, Mark, was a Central basketball assistant for a brief time and later became one of the most revered and beloved principals to ever work in the Mahomet-Seymour school district, retiring from Sangamon Elementary in 2017.

Glennon also went with me for what was the most memorable high school baseball game I covered.

It was a regional tournament semifinal, matching the Urbana Tigers with the Bloomington Purple Raiders.

Urbana sent a left-hander to the pitching mound, Darren Hursey. About 13 months after this particular Saturday afternoon game, Hursey was drafted by the Detroit Tigers. Soon after the draft, he signed a professional contract.

On this day, however, he pitched a seven-inning no-hitter and struck out 22 batters. He had to face one extra batter because a dropped third strike enabled one player to reach first base.

I've witnessed other no-hitters, but this was the most dominating performance I saw in person by a pitcher at the high school level.

Glennon was one of many outstanding individuals I had the privilege to work with during my years in the media business.

There was never a better gentleman than Emil Hesse, whose byline featured his initials, E.W.

He was an outside-of-the-box thinker as well as a beloved baseball fan. Long before The News-Gazette began producing what we referred to as All-Area teams, he recognized athletes in basketball at the end of each season.

He called his team the Elite Eight. He also picked a second team of eight.

His rationale for having eight players is that it coincided with the number of basketball teams that could earn state tournament berths in his era. Eight teams advanced to state and played in a quarterfinal round game.

The IHSA dubbed those qualifying schools the Elite Eight. Hesse liked that concept and borrowed it for his all-star team.

He was also a very precise writer and made sure every word meant something and wasn't there simply to fill space. As a result, he gave his stories careful consideration. Often times, the length of his stories would be shorter than many of the rest of us. That was because of the time required for him to polish his stories.

Another former News-Gazette colleague who made a dynamic impression was Jeff Pierron. I prided myself on a good work ethic, but Pierron showed me how to take that effort to another level, which I continued long after he left for greener pastures in Ohio.

Joe Millas was the person I was the closest with at The News-Gazette. We got to know each other well when we were technically competitors. He was writing for The News-Gazette and I was a fledgling reporter at the Champaign-Urbana Morning Courier.

We were both assigned to the Centennial High School beat and ran into each other at game after game. We quickly figured out it didn't make much sense for us to travel separately to the same location, so we began sharing rides.

I usually drove because I had access to a company car at The Courier. This was during the 1975-76 school year and there were no high-tech devices for us to use.

A typical out-of-town trip went like this: after the game ended, we hustled back to my car and started driving, keeping our eyes open for a gas station with an outdoor phone booth. We preferred one with two phone booths, but that was often too much to locate in an unfamiliar area.

One night after a football game on a rain-soaked field at Decatur Eisenhower High School, we found a gas station on the south end of town. I pulled in and parked. We spent a few minutes totaling up our game statistics and then alternated using the phone.

Joe went first and called his office, dictating his stats. He returned to the car and started writing his story out long-hand while I phoned in my stats. He finished his story and returned to the phone to dictate while I completed my story, writing it out on a yellow legal pad.

The rain was still pouring down as we sprinted from car to phone booth and back at Decatur. The absolute worst part is that the glass partition in the booth was broken and we were getting doused during the 15 minutes or so we spent in the booth talking to our people back at the office.

Though I sometimes get frustrated with modern technology when I can't get it to do what it was designed for, I much prefer the current system that was in place by my retirement.

The technology allowed me to travel to out-of-town games, cover the contest, conduct the interviews and return to a spot in the bleachers, open my laptop, connect to Wifi, write a story, hit a button and it would show up simultaneously in the appropriate file back at The News-Gazette headquarters.

Sometimes, I became panicked and it had nothing to do with technology. After a Friday night football game in Cerro Gordo, a janitor told me, "Lights off in five minutes and I'm going home."

The game had ended late and I had only been writing for

about five minutes. It was already nearly 10 p.m. I explained that I needed more time than five minutes and he responded, "Unless you authorize my overtime, we're both out of here in five minutes."

I'm sure my fingers never moved faster over a keyboard than they did that night. Combined with me stretching that five minutes into eight or nine minutes, I was able to finish my story. Barely.

Joe Millas was long gone from The Gazette by this time.

Joe and I wound up riding together for most of three school years in the 1970s.

When I arrived at The Gazette in 1981, I wound up with a desk directly across from his. Sometimes we had to be reminded that we were at the office to work. We both liked to talk about our stories, brainstorm, share ideas and make suggestions. He was a joy to be around.

One highlight was when Joe got remarried at his home in Mahomet in 1982 and asked me to stand up with him as his best man. I was honored to have a place by his side. If everybody had Joe's personality, the world would be a terrific place.

After leaving The News-Gazette, Joe devoted full-time to teaching.

The best sportswriter I've known personally is one I just missed working with. Doug Carroll left The News-Gazette shortly before I arrived. We'd gotten to know each other while I was at The Courier.

I marveled at how he could make any story interesting. I am convinced that he could write a riveting story about mowing your yard and it would keep a reader's attention until the last word.

I also believe if he saw a basketball game like I did in 1981, when the Sullivan girls won at Decatur St. Teresa, 116-16, he would produce an award-winning article. I truly believe that reading his stories was the inspiration I needed to always strive to better myself as a sports writer. He set the bar extremely high.

I don't think any newspaper has had anyone who was as much of an authority and a walking encyclopedia of knowledge on cross-country and track and field as David Woods. My former News-Gazette colleague was a hometown product who had information available at the snap of your fingers. Honestly, I relied on his expertise several times after he moved on from the Gazette to San Jose, Cal., and ultimately to Indianapolis (with a stop back at The Gazette in between).

One last News-Gazette tidbit. I discovered – quite by accident – that it's possible in your carelessness to give someone a nickname that sticks.

We had a top-notch photo staff throughout my tenure at The News-Gazette. I had the chance to work with all of them at one time or another, but because I was assigned to Vermilion County for most of the 1990s and photographer Rick Danzl was, too, we went to a lot of the same events.

One thing photo chief Darrell Hoemann knew for certain was that he didn't want a camera in my hands. I had a special knack for creating blurry photos or chopping off half of a person's head. So Danzl was with me repeatedly.

I always said – and meant it – that his picture drew people in to read my story. Sometimes, I even matched his quality of work.

Reporters are asked to write the cutlines – captions – for the pictures taken at events they cover because of having more information than is available to the copy editors. I did so dutifully one night, thought I proofread what I wrote and passed it onto the people doing the page design.

I assumed at least one other set of eyes would look at what I wrote.

The next day, I heard people talking in jest about our new photographer. It seems that I had inadvertently attributed the photo to Rock Danzl. And so, Rick became Rock, though never again in the newspaper!

I could name dozens of other talented writers and editors that we had at The Gazette – in all departments – but should move on to the other newspapers where I worked.

The crew I joined at The Pantagraph was much like me in terms of age. All of us in the sports department – except copy editor Tom Gumbrel – were either about to graduate from college or had done so very recently. Most of the sports staff was in our early to mid-20s.

Many of them were committed to the newspaper and stayed for decades. Bryan Bloodworth worked his way up to the sports editor position and when he left, was replaced by Randy Kindred, who was as affable as anyone I ever worked with. He was a voice of reason, whatever the situation.

Two other sportswriters from my time stayed at The Pantagraph for decades, but switched departments, Mark Lewis and Bill Flick.

Flick always had an interesting approach to things and ultimately found his niche as a columnist and humorist. His departure was certainly a loss for the sporting world. For years after I had moved on, I would go to the store and buy a copy of the newspaper on days I knew he was writing. That only stopped after every store in Mahomet, and then Mansfield, stopped carrying The Pantagraph.

What were they thinking?

I always found it funny that Bill's favorite ball team started with the same letter as his hometown. When you're from Olney, there aren't many possibilities to cheer for except the Orioles.

We must have had too much free time while I was in Bloomington. Flick and I fervently played a tabletop baseball game together, APBA. I was so addicted that I had APBA 1 as my license plate for at least a decade.

Perhaps the person I admired most for his writing skills and storytelling while I was at The Pantagraph was Mark Wellwood. He had a creative knack much like Doug Carroll and whenever I saw Wellwood's byline, I made his article the first one I would read. I was rarely disappointed.

Like so often happens, we went different ways and though I've wondered about him, we haven't been in contact for decades.

Most amazing was the sports department that worked out of The Courier office, on Race Street, in Urbana.

My impression – and circulation supported this – is that we were the No. 2 daily paper in the Twin Cities.

And yet …

Our sports editor, Lon Eubanks, went on to work at the Memphis Commercial Appeal.

One of the prep beat writers, Rick Vacek, moved to California and covered the Oakland A's in 1981 and '82 for the San Jose Mercury News. He continued moving up the newspaper ladder, spending four years as sports editor of the Los Angeles Daily News and later 18 months as the assistant managing editor of the Kansas City Star.

Another prep beat writer was Mike Babcock, who returned to Nebraska and authored a book on legendary football coach Tom Osborne's legacy, entitled "Heart of a Husker." He spent 17 years as a sportswriter at the Lincoln (Neb.) Journal Star. Among his writing credits is a book he co-authored on another legendary Cornhusker coach, Bob Devaney.

Paul Ayars, another brilliant wordsmith, became a long-time staff member at the Lincoln (Ill.) Courier. Mike VanAntwerp was a colleague who dabbled in the media for years after leaving The Courier.

Also working at The Courier was Carrie Muskat, who went on to cover the Chicago Cubs, starting in 2001 before retiring from MLB.dot after the 2018 season. She has written books on Barry Bonds, Sammy Sosa and Mark McGwire. Jeff Cade was another coveted part-timer between 1977-79. He stayed in the newspaper business more than a quarter of a century, with stints in Illinois at Belleville and Arlington Heights followed by four years at the San Diego Tribune and 17 years at the Arizona Republic.

Vacek, Babcock, VanAntwerp, Muskat, Cade and myself were all part-timers while at the Courier.

Three of the full-time writers, Dave French, Wally Haas and Reed Schreck, all wound up in Rockford, working for the Register Star. Haas started in sports and now serves as the editorial page editor. He won an award from the Associated Press in 2018 for his work. Schreck retired earlier this decade after covering prep sports in the community for two decades and serving as the newspaper's NFL reporter. French, who is deceased, was also at the paper for years, before relocating to Florida.

It is amazing to think about the level of talent that was at The Courier in the middle 1970s.

And that doesn't even begin to touch on the other departments. Phil Greer was a top-flight photographer who went directly from The Courier (where he spent 12 years) to the Chicago Tribune where he worked for another 24 years, eventually serving as director of photography. Greer was nominated multiple times for the Pulitzer Prize in Journalism.

That Courier photo staff also included Curt Beamer, Lou McClellan, Gene Suggs and Jerry Lower, all of whom were true artists with a camera. When you can't do something, you learn to appreciate those who can.

What a treat it was for me to have been associated with so many talented and terrific people.

Like myself, Lower was a Mahomet-Seymour graduate as was Bret Beherns, who worked part time at The News-Gazette before turning his focus to television and a long career as sports director at WCIA, in Champaign. Another WCIA on-air personality, Aaron Eades, is also a Mahomet-Seymour graduate. Jim Johnston, a news photographer in Indianapolis, used to call Mahomet home.

Hans Waters – a former captain on the M-S cross-country team – has two Emmys for his work as a freelance video editor specializing in sports broadcasts. Among his myriad credits are Final Fours, the Olympics and Super Bowls. He has done work for both CBS and NBC.

Patrick Quinn, a former Bulldog football letterman, has done public relations work, TV work and classroom instruction.

Quinn's TV news career has taken him to locations such as Fort Myers, Champaign, West Palm Beach, Cleveland and Milwaukee as well as the St. Louis area. He has been working at KMOV News 4 (a CBS Affiliate) as a News Producer and Assignment Editor. He also teaches a journalism class at Lindenwood University. Quinn has done voiceovers for Illini basketball and football commercials on central Illinois radio stations.

There are so many former M-S students that are or have been involved in some form of media or communications – and probably others whom I have inadvertently overlooked – that it's easy to see why there is a Hometown Proud feeling throughout the community.

One of the first people I met outside of the sports department at the Bloomington Daily Pantagraph was Bill Wills, an early 1960s M-S graduate. He was a city editor at the newspaper for decades.

I consider myself surrounded by outstanding company.

Fred's Favorites

FAVORITE TEACHERS
1. Linda Cooper (high school journalism)
2. Jean Thompson (college rhetoric)
3. Geralyn Koeberlein (high school mathematics)
4. Margaret Rinkel (high school English)
5. Jerry Huffington (high school agriculture)
6. Larry Gnagey (band, role model)

CHAPTER TWENTY-ONE

The toughest job I ever had was one where I didn't receive any monetary compensation.

That's OK, being a parent had plenty of other rewards and perks.

I entered into parenthood without a strong foundation of what to expect. I felt my own childhood was unfulfilled and one I wouldn't want anyone else to duplicate. So, I didn't.

That was, in fact, my starting point.

Many decisions about my son Devin were made based on whether it was the opposite of the standards that were applied to me while I was being raised.

He was on a plane, headed to a vacation destination before he was six-months old. I'm sure he has no memory of that particular Florida trip, but he later told me he counted his trips to Disney World and he had been there 12 times by the time he graduated from high school.

As for activities, I didn't push any upon him, but encouraged him to make decisions on what to pursue based on actual knowledge of what they were like and what they entailed.

He played T-ball and then one year of coach-pitch baseball

before deciding he didn't like the idea of balls being thrown at him.

A year of flag football was all he needed to abandon that sport.

He developed a liking to soccer and played on rec teams from first grade through eighth grade. Basketball was another passion, and he played on intramural teams throughout high school.

It wasn't all about sports. Devin was in Cub Scouts and 4-H. He really liked working with and showing horses. He had a special pony, Smokey, that was his pride and joy.

He also showed an Appaloosa, Our Independence (so named because of being born on the Fourth of July), and we traveled a wide circuit in the summer, not just throughout Illinois, but multiple trips to Oklahoma City (we were there a few months after the 1995 bombing took place) and Houston, Texas.

Many of the ventures with horses were made with our trainer, Peggy Redding, her husband, Kirk, and their daughters, Staci and Stefanie. The socialization and time together were as important as the ribbons won, at least in my mind.

During junior high, Devin participated on the speech team. He not only enjoyed it, but also did well.

Though Devin is my only biological child – a lonely status I considered one of the greatest problems with my childhood – I justified this because he wasn't denied opportunities to be active in endeavors of his choice. And, even though we lived in a rural area for the majority of his childhood, we made sure that wasn't an excuse to prevent him from participating as much as if he lived in town.

He wasn't stuck in the country with nothing to do but entertain himself. He wasn't required to wait until he was an adult to travel and see the world.

He went with me to dozens of basketball games, too, both during the school year and during the summer months.

His high school career had several parallels to mine. The school newspaper, which I had helped restart as a junior in the fall of 1971 (The Bulldog Journal), had gone by the wayside again by 2000. Devin helped revive it when he was a junior and he, too, served as the editor.

He did commentary on basketball games for MySchoolWorld.com while in high school, learning how to produce the show as well as handling on-air interviews and game play-by-play commentary.

He was also writing weekly sports roundups for the Mahomet Citizen. We spent many Sunday afternoons working on his copy and perfecting his content. I derived as much enjoyment from helping him as I did in developing my own stories for The News-Gazette.

Though I had an infinite amount of pride in his writing and reporting skills, one of my happiest days was when I learned he wasn't planning on pursuing a career in newspapering. It went beyond the uncertain future for the industry or the inordinate amount of night-time work hours required.

Whatever the occupation, I think it is extremely tough for a child to follow in the footsteps of a parent who has been in the same profession and experienced a degree of success. I've seen the unwarranted and – sometimes – unrealistic expectations, based not on the potential of the young person, but rather on the performance of the older one.

There are no clones, and each person should be judged solely on what they can do, not on what the family has achieved or what society thinks they should do. Devin would have made a fine journalist, but I was pleased to see him make a name for himself in another area.

Like me, Devin knew at a young age what he wanted to do.

Devin Kroner, December, 1984 age 1 1/2.

Devin Kroner with his pony, Smokey, undated.

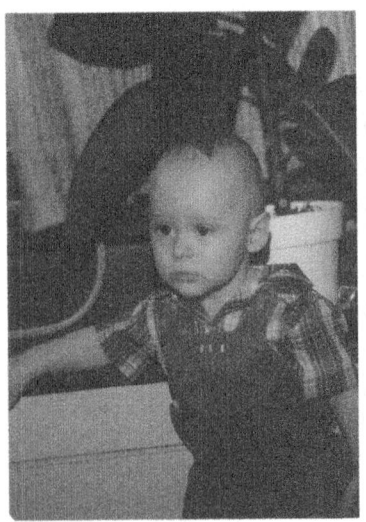

Devin Kroner 1984.

Devin Kroner, September, 2002, age 18, senior year.

As a high school freshman, he told me he wanted to get into the ministry. Like me, he followed through on his dreams. For him, that meant going directly to Rhema Bible College, in Tulsa, Okla., after high school.

In my mind, the newspaper writing he did was a benefit when it came time to put together weekly sermons as he advanced to serving a church of his own. He knew how to organize and structure what he wanted to say. He learned to make a point, elaborate and support the point, and to recognize that there are always two ways to look at issues.

Plus, he adds a touch of humor now and then to keep everyone listening.

One thing he definitely didn't get from me was the ability to feel comfortable speaking in front of crowds, no matter how large. I do best when I have ample time to contemplate the next word or the next sentence.

There are sentences in this book that have taken me 15 minutes to write.

Extemporaneous speaking is not my forte, but Devin is not only unfazed by it, but he also seems to flourish when these opportunities arise. I've heard this from enough other people that I don't think those are merely the thoughts of an ultra-proud parent.

As much as I would like to take credit for Devin turning out to be a kind-hearted, generous, gracious, respectful and industrious young man, the truth rests elsewhere.

By the time he was a teen-ager, I was separated from his mother, Dee. We later divorced. She had primary responsibility for his care and upbringing throughout the high school years. She deserves credit for keeping things together during a tumultuous time; a time when teen-agers face so many options and distractions and can take their lives in any number of directions.

I don't hesitate in saying – and meaning – that she was a better mother than I was a father.

In the meantime, I had three bonus children come into my life when I married Emily Moon, whom I had known for decades. Salim Belahi was out of high school and Jamel Belahi was entering into his senior year when Emily and I got together.

Emily moved back to Mahomet to be with me. Salim and Jamel both stayed in Florida at that time. Their youngest sibling, Malika Belahi, joined us in Mahomet for her final five years of schooling.

It was my first – and only – experience ever having a young lady in the house and it went better than I could have imagined, but I suspect that has more to do with Malika than with me.

As the years passed, all of Emily's children lived with us for a time. Two of them liked the area enough that they have taken up permanent residence in Champaign County. Jamel is not a cold-weather fan, and relocated back to Florida, in the Ormond Beach area where he was raised.

In what must be considered an ironic twist, the two adult children who lived the closest have no children while the two who live the furthest are each raising at least three children.

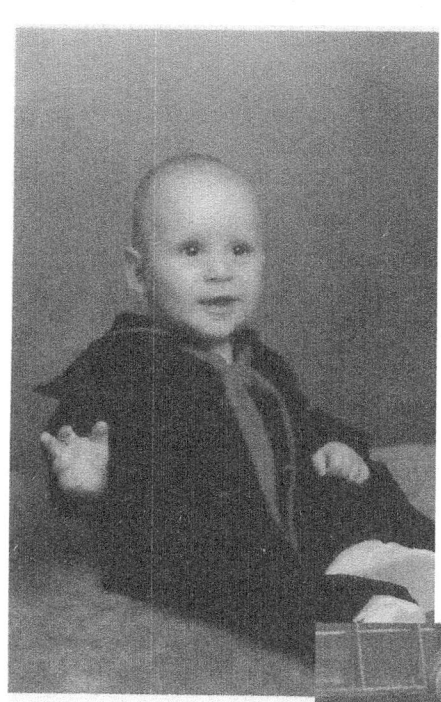

Devin Kroner,
December, 1983,
age 9 months.

Cowboy Devin Kroner.

CHAPTER TWENTY-TWO

Calendar year 2018 marked a significant one for me, one which I didn't realize was upon me until I actually did the math.

That year was my 50th writing for a newspaper. I started out working for a weekly, evolved into dailies and am winding up with an on-line only publication, Mahomet Daily.

It has been quite the ride.

Fred Kroner in a News-Gazette car, driving to Peoria for the state softball tournament, May, 2012.

Doing some rough calculations, I figure I have produced in the neighborhood of 17,000 byline stories as Year 51 draws to a close. I've traveled well over a million miles in more of my own cars than I care to remember, plus a few company-owned vehicles.

Most stories I don't even remember, including ones which were nominated for and received recognition in national sportswriting contests. I'm the person who would learn about a story faring well with the judges and then ask the sports editor which story it was that had been submitted.

It was not something which I paid much attention to.

I can recall the people I wrote about much better than what words I penned about them.

There's one noteworthy exception.

There's a particular story that I vividly remember and likely will never forget. Of the 17,000-plus, it's the most memorable one for me personally, which is why it is the only full story I'm sharing in this book from my days working for daily newspapers.

It was published in the Champaign-Urbana News-Gazette on Wednesday, Nov. 30, 2005, starting on the front page of the sports section under the headline, "It's back to school again – for a memorable learning experience"

The story:

KANKAKEE – A wily coach once listened as a fledgling reporter – myself – marveled at the seemingly spectacular feats during a game that just ended.

When I finished – and editorialized that surely he'd never witnessed anything like that before – the veteran coach remarked, "When you've been around as long as I have, you've seen everything at least once and most things twice."

On Monday, I was able to witness another first. The expectation as I drove to the gymnasium was merely to watch the varsity coaching debut for my son, Devin, who has both the boys' and girls' basketball teams at Buckley Christ Lutheran, a high school in Iroquois County with a total enrollment of 25.

WHAT A SITE

Sure enough, that purpose was fulfilled, but this night would have been memorable regardless of who was coaching or the outcome.

Christ Lutheran lost the boys' game by six points and – thankfully – the coach received no technical fouls.

The opponent, Kankakee Trinity, plays its home games at the old National Guard Armory, now renamed the Community Resource Center. The scene was reminiscent of a Saturday morning park district game for third-graders.

There were no locker rooms, so the 10 Christ Lutheran athletes were obliged to change in the public restroom.

There was no scoreboard or clock inside the gymnasium except what was in front of the official timer. When there were 10 seconds left in a quarter, he'd start a countdown to zero.

The players shot not at goals attached to a wall (or a permanent fixture), but to the portable variety found in many backyards, the kind that can be slid away quickly to make room for the soccer goals which were stashed in one corner.

Without locker rooms, the players remained on the court for halftime and listened to the coach from what was truly a bench – an eight-foot long wooden variety that probably would have been state-of-the-art when some of the great-grandfathers of today's players were in high school.

The start of the boys' varsity game was delayed because a junior high contest was still in progress at the scheduled time for the high school matchup. When the main attraction got under way, the same referees who worked the earlier youth game remained for another 32 minutes of action.

Without a flag in the gym, there was no pregame National

Anthem or even the Pledge of Allegiance. Instead, the game was preceded by a prayer.

Fans in the stands not only had no concession stand available on the premises, but had difficulty finding an unobstructed view of the court. Four pillars are located in front of the seating areas on each side, creating blind spots where the athletes literally disappear in front of your eyes for a few seconds.

It was in this setting that Devin Kroner – attired in his nicest suit – started his coaching career after commenting, "I'm halfway between excited and scared to death."

At least he was honest.

ROLE REVERSAL

So, how does this work?

That thought crossed my mind repeatedly. Throughout my soon-to-be 25-year tenure at The News-Gazette, I've witnessed an average of more than 100 prep basketball games a year. And yet, never was there occasion to interview a coach I helped raise.

There was that time in 1984 when a newspaper colleague – the esteemed Ed Glennon – was mistaken for the brother I never had, but other than that, the only family ties in the workplace were the ones I occasionally wore around my neck.

Do I start a postgame interview like I would with former Danville coach Gene Gourley – whom I have known longer than Devin has been alive – or do I give this coach a hug and tell him how proud I am that his team looked organized and disciplined (usually) and had fought the good fight?

I did neither, letting the moment pass so he could have time with his team. When we found ourselves together, it was the coach who started the questioning.

"What did you think?" he asked.

That query presented a new and intriguing dilemma. Is the

interviewer suddenly being interviewed? Do I answer like a stereotypical parent and quote a cliché like, "You can't win them all?" or do I offer an analytical perspective that 2 ½ decades of watching this wonderful game as a sportswriter has afforded me:

"There were too many possessions where it was one pass and a shot, where they settled for a three, where they didn't crash the boards, where they rushed their shot on a layup, where…"

Before any response was made, I recalled the free advice coaches are always receiving from well-intentioned fans and decided this youthful coach could see those details for himself by studying the game film.

"You'll never forget this night," the reporter said to the coach. And with that, the father and the son went their separate ways, with at least one of them thinking, "Now, I really have seen everything."

Fred Kroner is the News-Gazette's prep sports coordinator. He writes a weekly column on high school athletics throughout the school year.

***

The Christ Lutheran boys' team finished the season with a record of 9-13. The girls' team ended with a record of 4-19.

The boys' school record for wins in a season is 10.

The girls' season was remarkable for one reason: every game was played with five players.

When it came time for the team's Feb. 6 regional opener, Christ Lutheran was in danger of having to forfeit.

One of its five players, Gracie Rosales, had been injured and was ruled out of the game. The IHSA allows teams to finish games with fewer than five players on the court, but schools are not allowed to have fewer than five on the court when the opening tip is held.

Junior Rachel Hoopingarner – who had played basketball the previous year – agreed to suit up against Gibson City-Melvin-Sibley even though she had not participated in any practices.

She played all 32 minutes and had eight rebounds and five blocked shots.

The girls' players made it clear that they appreciated the chance to play the games.

Cory Kurowski told a newspaper reporter after a late-season game, "We come in with the mindset every game we can do it, though it's very tough. I'm just glad we have a team."

That year was my son's only one as head coach. The following summer, he moved to Tennessee to pursue opportunities in the ministry and has since relocated to Kansas, Michigan and Kentucky.

For my part, I didn't officially cover any of his team's other games, but took several nights off to see the Crusaders play.

I thoroughly enjoyed the fan-in-the-stands role.

Devin Kroner and Fred Kroner, undated.

A random car at the state softball tournament, but not belonging to Fred Kroner.

Fred Kroner, finishing a story at Palmer Arena, Danville, after the crowds are gone.

CHAPTER TWENTY-THREE

There's a large group of former area athletes who resurfaced as area head coaches.

It was been a neat perk for me to follow these individuals from the times they were being coached to the times they were doing the coaching.

Westville's Joe Brazas is prominent in that group. As a high school senior in 1995, he was a three-sport all-conference first-team selection in football, basketball and baseball for the Tigers.

He returned to his alma mater in 2003 as an assistant in boys' basketball and five years later became the Tigers' varsity baseball head coach.

The period in between his stint as an athlete and his tenure as a coach is what stands out.

When he committed to Parkland College for baseball, we talked about his goals and aspirations.

"I would love to play major league baseball," he said. "That's definitely a goal I am shooting for."

After playing baseball for two years at Parkland College, Brazas transferred in 1997 to Berry College in Georgia.

Less than a month after he arrived in the state, his car was hit broadside by a teen-aged driver on Sept. 9, 1997.

He suffered a traumatic brain injury, was in a coma for six days and was paralyzed on his right side.

The first memory, when he awoke, was "a scary thing," he said. "My right side wouldn't move at all."

His collegiate baseball career was over.

The first good sign was when he sneezed and "my right arm moved," Brazas said, "but the doctor said it was involuntary."

For 20 days, he was hospitalized in Georgia, then flown to Champaign where he was admitted to Covenant Medical Center.

His parents graciously allowed me to be at the hospital during some of his seven-daily 30-minute therapy sessions. On Oct. 2, 1997, I witnessed what would have been considered a miracle three weeks earlier.

With physical therapists holding onto each arm, Brazas took a step on his own.

His right arm and right leg still had no feeling, but he was able to move forward by dragging the foot.

That was the beginning of a six-year journey that I consider the most heart-warming story I've had the privilege to cover.

In those six years, he completed rehab, completed his college degree at Eastern Illinois University and immediately returned to the classroom as a science, health and driver's education teacher at Westville High School.

Shortly after his hiring, he told me, "Everyone thought I was down and out. I had a desire to do something. I did it to prove I could do it."

Brazas has made adjustments. He learned to write left-handed and opens doors with his left hand.

"I've gotten to where I can run, but not like I used to," he said. "I'd say I'm about 75 percent back."

He's 100 percent grateful.

"I am thankful for so much," Brazas said. "Everything is going well.

"I'm fortunate. When I wake up in the morning I don't go, 'Ugh, I've got to go to work.' I enjoy what I do."

He particularly likes coaching baseball, though the former power pitcher has made one concession.

"I never throw batting practice," Brazas said. "I can't throw like I used to. Sometimes we have someone else throw or we use the pitching machine."

It's the best comeback I personally witnessed while on the job.

I was most appreciative that Joe Brazas and another veteran Westville coach, Jeff Millis, took time out of their schedules to attend my retirement party from The News-Gazette in June, 2015 at the UI's Memorial Stadium.

In my mind, Millis is the master of coaching the fundamentals of basketball, just like another long-time Vermilion County coach, Randy Skaggs, was at teaching the strategies and situations in baseball and softball. They are two of the best at their craft that I encountered at the high school level.

Their players were well-tutored in the fundamentals of the game and in why things are done as they are.

CHAPTER TWENTY-FOUR

No matter how much planning – or wishing – a person does, sometimes the key is simply being in the right place at the right time.

Occasionally, those moments piggyback on each other.

For years, my wife Emily and I have enjoyed going to open houses, even if we had no intention of buying, because we like to see the insides of houses we've only seen from the outside.

We went to one open house in early summer of 2004. The draw was that it was one of the older homes in Mahomet, having been built in 1872. It was originally the home of the Thomas Scott family.

We marveled at how well preserved it was and how well it held up over time. Then, we left on vacation, assuming it would soon be snapped up.

After returning home 10 days later, we noticed not only that it was still for sale, but also that another open house was scheduled for the upcoming Sunday. Having nothing else to do that afternoon, we dropped by for another look.

We were living on Division St. at the time, in a home that had been in my family since the 1930s. There was no dissatisfaction with it, nor were we looking to move.

But still, we decided to make an offer for the property, located right along Rt. 150. Our offer was for less than the asking price, and we felt confident it wouldn't be accepted.

The realtor called the next day and wondered if we had all of our financing in place. I had to scurry around to make things happen. It turns out the owners took our offer.

In September of 2004, we made what we hope will be our final move.

Fred and Emily Kroner, January, 2019.

As we got accustomed to the neighborhood, we discovered a tiny, quaint building just to the west of our home. It was a coffee shop at the time.

Emily remarked that it would be the perfect size (504-square feet) and site for a bakery, which happens to be one of her multitudes of interests. Not immediately, but within the first year at our new location, we learned the name of the building owner and contacted her, to let her know if the property ever became available, we would be interested in renting it.

A decade passed, and life continued. Emily had a handful of clients who asked her to make sweet or savory items and she fixed them out of our home, without advertising.

In January, 2017, we found out that the Coffee Station owner, Ron Sebestik, was retiring and the building would soon be vacant. The building owner still remembered us from when we had contacted her previously, and we quickly agreed to terms.

We took over the building in February, 2017, and with the assistance of Thomas McMahon, who made the needed fix-up work a priority, everything was up and running by July, 2017.

We received the required permits from the Champaign County Health Department and opened for business on Saturday, July 15, 2017.

The nice thing about the first day is that we had already determined to be closed on Sundays and Mondays, so that gave us time to evaluate and assess what we were doing without the pressure of being open while working through some of the opening-day kinks.

Emily chose the name, Lucky Moon Pies & More, as a tribute to her maiden name (Moon). The "& More" was added so that we could incorporate cakes, brownies, cookies, tarts, cake pops, bars and dog treats into our menu lineup, which changes from day to day.

Thanks to suggestions from customers, within a few months of opening, the "& More" also included a savory item each of the five days we're open. Some days, the savory is the most popular selection.

The "Lucky" in the title was necessary to avoid confusion with a treat (Moon Pies) created in the early 1900s. Even with what we thought were adequate precautions, three or four people a year come in and ask to see, "a moon pie."

My role at the pie shop – in my opinion – is the best one of all. I get to meet and greet customers at the register as I ring up orders and I am able to serve as the official taste-tester.

After all, we wouldn't want to send sub-quality products out the door.

At times, it's necessary to re-do the test to make sure my first impression was accurate!

I enjoy my volunteer job for reasons that are difficult to explain, but which make perfect sense to me.

An ex-wife once told me she grew tired of going somewhere with me only to hear some random person come up and compliment me for a story I had written for the newspaper.

"I'm as good at my job as you are at yours," she said, "but I don't get the kudos and slaps on the back that you get because I'm not out in the public."

I tried, to no avail, to explain that I didn't seek the recognition and couldn't control what people said or when they said it.

Any praise directed to the pie shop is not a reflection on me. It's totally based on Emily and the super staff she has assembled. I like that.

I also love how well-received her venture has been. Lucky Moon Pies & More had been in business less than a year when it was voted the runner-up in the category of "pies" by the people who participated in the annual News-Gazette Reader's Choice awards in 2018.

A few months thereafter, recognition followed from the Mahomet Area Chamber of Commerce for first place in the "Start-Up Business of the Year" category.

And in 2019, Lucky Moon Pies & More was voted in "The best of 217" as the No. 1 bakery within that area code.

The News-Gazette conducted a reader's poll again in 2019 and Lucky Moon Pies & More placed second in the newspaper's vast circulation area for pies.

At an age when many people are thinking only about retiring and decreasing their workload, Emily embraced becoming a first-time business owner with employees and created a successful and thriving establishment right out of the gate.

All of these tributes and honors arrived within the first 24 months of opening.

It makes me proud.

From left, Mike Hulvey, Emily Kroner, Fred Kroner and Scott Eisenhauer.

CHAPTER TWENTY-FIVE

I've interviewed lawyers and doctors, bankers and teachers, nurses and engineers.

I've spoken to six-year-olds at the conclusion of an age-group swimming meet and 70-year-olds after the last out in a rec league championship softball game.

I've been there to see the best moments for people, immediately after capturing a state title, and the worst moments, as they share their feelings and memories after a loved one has unexpectedly passed away.

I've talked with baseball greats: Henry Aaron, Billy Williams and Pete Rose as well as the last-place finisher in a girls' high school cross-country race.

In the words of former Danville Area Community College men's basketball coach John Spezia, "you're everywhere."

Many of my personal highlights, however, took place long after the athletes I covered were finished with their competitive careers.

Very few games remain crystal clear in my memory bank, but the people who played in them or coached them are still very prominent.

It's getting an invitation to ex-Unity athlete Maggie

Hauser's wedding and knowing that in 2019, she was enshrined in her high school's Hall of Fame.

It's getting a call from former Olympic speedskater Erik Henriksen the night his father, Harry, passed because he needed to talk.

It's being asked by Karen Bloch to be her presenter for her induction into the Danville Area Community College Hall of Fame.

Fred Kroner and Karen Bloch, June 2015.

It's seeing Roger McClendon 34 years after he graduated from Centennial High School and talking about events like they had happened a week earlier.

It's seeing one-time Shiloh High School standout Taylor Hawkins Frick when it's time to get a haircut and noticing a framed story I had written, on the wall next to a mirror at her business.

It's knowing that someone like Tyke Peacock, a state

champion high jumper from Urbana, had the confidence and trust in me to tell his moving story, a tale about an athlete who was literally on top of the world before falling to the deepest depths possible due to drug use and then pulling himself together to be an inspiration for others.

It's hearing from former Milford prep Shannon Garrelts Muench as she offered thanks for the support I provided during her tough times.

It's a call from Les Hoveln, wondering if I have still access to his career baseball stats from when he played for Royal's Eastern Illinois Baseball League entry.

It's former Sullivan basketball All-Stater Becky Clayton Anderson calling to say, "Hi. How are you doing?"

It's a random message from former Jamaica girls' basketball assistant Barry Eakle asking if I'm available for lunch.

It's this and so much more.

It's the people, none of whom I would have ever met in the first place had I not been assigned at some point to watch them or their teams play.

Journalism has been an interesting profession. We'd like to think we make a difference and provide an accurate keepsake with our stories, yet we seldom receive verification.

During my time at The News-Gazette, we had upwards of 40,000 subscribers for many years. A typical article might generate one or two responses and those generally came from people with a complaint or who wanted to point out an error.

My colleagues and I would joke that if we heard from three people criticizing a story, then 39,997 must have liked it. That made us feel good, and gave us a laugh, even though the reality is probably more like 39,990 truly didn't care one way or another, or hadn't even read the article.

The moments that happen years later are significant, hearing about what the athlete has been doing since graduating from high school. When you're watching students from nearly 50 high schools and 20 different sports for three-plus decades, that leaves a potential list in the thousands that you wonder what they became, what they are doing, where they are living.

I love reunions. I love Hall-of-Fame gatherings. I love reconnecting on Facebook. These vehicles bring people together and are a chance to catch up.

Annie Parrett Schnepper graduated from Centennial High School in 2003. The next time I saw her was 16 years later when she was inducted into her high school's Hall of Fame.

It was no longer an adult talking to a teen-ager asking for perspective and comments about a game played. It was one adult talking to another, not in an interview situation, but as a chance to reminisce.

Childhood friends are special because – in many cases – I knew them for all 12 years I was in school. But their numbers tend to dwindle. Rick Durst is no longer with us. Neither is Jeff Hinton. Or Rick Stauffer. Or Greg Brown. Or more than a dozen others who graduated with me in 1973.

Walter Pierce is someone I still see weekly. And, I'm in touch with other former classmates such as Galen Dale, Robert Herbst, Holmes Kimble, Bill Murphy, Terry Shoemaker and Brad Stipp on a regular basis.

Beyond that, many of the people I am closest to are either ones I worked with over the years or are former athletes and coaches who have made an effort to stay in touch even after I am no longer writing about them.

The Bloch family, of Oreana, started including me in family functions such as Thanksgiving and Christmas gatherings a quarter of a century ago. Matriarch Sandy and her daughters Karen and Katie and daughter-in-law Radena confirmed my feeling that I totally missed out by not having siblings.

They are all as genuinely sweet as anyone you will find and I always look forward, with great anticipation, to our next gathering.

From left, Katie Bloch, Sandy Bloch, Sydney Bloch, Kandie Bloch, Fred Kroner, Karen Bloch and Radena Lemmon.

I think these and other friendships happened and were built for one reason. I never, ever, looked at my job as one of simply documenting a sports game and detailing all of the action.

I focused on the people, dug deep into their personalities and learned about who they were as individuals. I shared as much about them as I did the game.

Re-reading some of my game accounts, I see it's not unusual to have only a few paragraphs highlighting the action on the field or on the court or the ball diamond. This approach takes work.

You don't just walk up to someone and say, "Tell me your life story."

You get to know people over a period of time. You show that you care and are fair. You become comfortable with them and they become confident in you. You gain a mutual trust with each other and the end result is an inside profile on a person, or a group, which would not otherwise be possible.

This was never really part of a master plan. It was me being myself and treating others with the respect and compassion I would like to receive if the roles were reversed.

Some of my greatest long-time personal associations became possible after meeting people while on the job.

There is not a finer person in the media business than Mike Hulvey, who got his start at radio station WDAN, in Danville, and is now the Chief Operating Officer for the entire Neuhoff Communications company, which owns and operates 23 radio stations in Illinois and Indiana.

Mike first got me on the air in 1994 as a guest on WDAN's weekly Saturday morning sports talk show. He couldn't get rid of me, even after I retired from being a full-time journalist and, 25 years after I started, I still make an appearance the majority of the 52 weeks in a year.

Through Mike, my wife and I got to know his wife Julie and their former Danville neighbors, Beth and John Lashbrook. We get together as regularly as our collective schedules allow for meals and conversation. The Hulveys and the Kroners – along with one of the longest active basketball coaches I know, John Spezia, took a trip to Antigua together and worked a basketball clinic and media camp while there.

Spezia is the epitome of the term "lifer" when it comes to coaching basketball.

Hulvey and former Danville mayor Scott Eisenhauer provided the impetus for starting an annual Sports Media Camp for Kids at DACC. It is a special week each June that had gained national exposure even before a young man from the state of Vermont, Jackson Evans, started attending. I volunteered regularly during the first two decades of the camp's existence, focusing on the newspaper portion of the program. This hands-on camp has included trips to St. Louis and Indianapolis, interviews with nationally-known sports personalities and the chance to do live broadcasts of Danville Dans baseball games.

I've lost track of how many former campers eventually found a job in sports media, but it was more than three dozen by 2015. Many of these individuals had their interest sparked at an early age, attending camp for the first time as seventh-graders.

Spezia is a person who needs no introduction. The IBCA Hall-of-Famer has coached all levels of basketball during his 40 years on the sidelines, including high school, junior college, professional and, in 2019, as the Antigua Men's National Team head coach.

The best Spezia story ever is courtesy of Mike Hulvey, who featured the coach on many of the Saturday sports talk shows during Spezia's 24-year tenure at Danville Area Community College.

Hulvey nicknamed Spezia "Coffee and Doughnuts."

The explanation: "You could ask John a question," Hulvey said, "then go out for coffee and doughnuts, and he would still be talking when you got back."

Spezia is a demanding coach. After one particularly frustrating road game while at DACC, he gathered his squad in Mary Miller Gymnasium after their return and conducted a practice session that extended past the midnight hour.

I believe there is only so much a person can remember and retain. I covered multiple state championship teams, but I don't recall scores for any of those games.

In truth, that's not what was important.

The players, the coaches and their euphoria, still makes me smile. I remember them vividly. I hope they feel the same way when they look back at their scrapbooks.

My many media colleagues as well are not only good people, but also good friends.

Fred's Favorites

FAVORITE VACATIONS I'VE TAKEN

1. San Diego
2. Nokomis, Fla.
3. Sydney, Australia
4. Toronto
5. Maui
6. Beijing

CHAPTER TWENTY-SIX

What are we without memories?

    I've had more than my share, many of which have been chronicled while telling my story.

There are others which are too precious to overlook, even though they won't fill a chapter by themselves.

I'll handle this as a question-and-answer with myself.

First, that reminds me of a series of columns E.W. Hesse authored on occasion. They would start, "Hey, E.W., what do you think about…"

Here are my answers to questions I might have been asked:

Q – Who were your favorites athletes to cover based on their names?

A – Three stand out equally, so I will list them alphabetically: Rose Dust (Unity), Nicke Nacke (Arcola) and Brandi Stein (Buckley-Loda).

Q – What was your toughest assignment?

A – The one that stands out is the first soccer match I covered. It was the first soccer match I'd ever seen, either in person or on television.

It was the first year that Champaign-Urbana high schools added the sport to their list of fall activities for boys.

Centennial High School was the first with a home match, and I was there. The date was Sept. 23, 1985. It was a Monday.

I started by doing what I've always done for football games: I walked the sidelines as the Chargers played Blue Mound, and followed the action. I probably didn't actually follow the action, but I watched.

At some point early in the match, a man approached me and thanked me for being at the historic match.

John Alumbaugh introduced himself and said if he could be of assistance to let him know. He was then the principal at Jefferson Middle School, which is located next door to Centennial High School.

I immediately took him up on the offer, acknowledging I had no background in soccer and asked if he could explain the reason for some of the whistles I was hearing.

Alumbaugh hung with me for the remainder of the match, updating me on what was taking place, explaining what the teams were trying to do and giving me a very general understanding of the game.

I'm sure my story didn't sound like it was written by an expert. I can only hope it didn't sound like it was written by a person who was clueless.

Centennial defeated Blue Mound, 5-1, in one of the nine matches the school played in its inaugural season. Jason Chicoine scored the first goal and Greg Endress was credited with the first assist ever in Champaign-Urbana prep soccer history.

In subsequent years, I ran into Alumbaugh frequently in soccer matches which I covered where he was a referee and at various Mahomet-Seymour events after he became the school district's superintendent in 1994, a position he held for 12 years.

Q – What is the top individual performance that you ever covered?

A – In another chapter, I talked about the baseball game where Urbana baseball pitcher Darren Hursey struck out 22 batters in a seven-inning game.

Another major moment was on Sept. 4, 1992 when I watched Danville's Travis Schofield score seven goals in an 11-0 soccer win over Westville at Danville's Whitesell Field. That mark remains the school record in 2019.

A 1993 graduate, Schofield amassed 109 goals in his four-year career, also an active school record.

Q – Were there any stories that made you laugh?

A – That's an interesting choice of words. One made me snicker. Literally. During Lon Henderson's tenure as girls' basketball coach at Danville High School in the 1990s, he grew tired of his players missing free throws due to lack of concentration.

He put out a challenge for his players to make four in a row, no matter how many games it took, and he would reward them with a free Snickers candy bar.

I became aware of this by hearing the bench shout, "Snickers," at various times in different games I was covering. Naturally, I wrote a story about this. I loved the stories that were not the typical run-of-the-mill kind.

Henderson got a copy of the article and, in turn, mailed it to the company which manufactured Snickers (Mars, Inc.) The company liked the publicity which had been generated and sent Henderson a couple of cases of the candy.

I will neither confirm nor deny that I might have eaten one.

Q –What is the most unusual thing you have seen in your years in sports?

A – Two come to mind, but the first wasn't anything I wrote about.

I was a high school sophomore at the time and took note that one of Mahomet-Seymour's junior basketball players, Steve Rinkel, used a jump shot to shoot free throws during a portion of the season when he was struggling with his shot. I don't recall seeing that again.

The other thing was about as rare.

I've seen several girls join high school football teams, but none made the impact that Janelle Hensold did for Danville.

She made 14 of 21 extra-point attempts for Danville's 2007 playoff team.

She became the first girl in school history to score a point in a football game in a 33-15 loss to Bloomington on Sept. 7, 2007. Her extra point attempt wasn't routine. Due to a penalty, her historic first point was a 25-yard kick.

Hensold also had a key role in a 35-34 homecoming win over Decatur MacArthur on Oct. 5, 2007. She hit 3 of 4 extra-point attempts in a game where the spectator turnout was reported at 3,200.

Q – Who were some of the best all-around high school female athletes you saw, over a period of time?

A – Two come immediately to mind.

Prairie Central's Melanie Ward was the first to earn News-Gazette All-Area first-team honors in three sports in the same school year, gaining recognition in volleyball, basketball and softball as a senior in 1990-91. Ward wound up playing basketball at Illinois State University.

Westville's Terra Ramsey took that success to a new level. As a sophomore in 2004-05, she was an All-Area first-team selection in softball in the spring. She followed up with All-Area first-team designations for all three sports she played as a junior and all three as a senior.

Ramsey wound up playing volleyball, basketball and softball at Danville Area Community College. She was an All-Area first-team pick in high school for an unprecedented seven consecutive sports seasons.

That record may prove as unbreakable as Cy Young's 511 career wins as a major league baseball pitcher.

Q – What is the most unique interview you conducted?

A – Two are equally memorable.

The first was when I reached former Argenta-Oreana athlete Jeff Blackard (a 1977 graduate) by phone and asked if he had a few minutes to talk.

He responded: "I'm driving to a meeting. I can talk until I get there."

The 1996 interview, while he was in Texas, was the first where I was aware of speaking to someone by cell phone while they were in transit.

The second was in 2011 when I needed to reach Westville football coach Guy Goodlove. I called his cell number one afternoon in the fall and reached him immediately.

We talked for a few minutes, then he asked me to hold on and I heard some yelling in the background. I asked what was going on and he explained he was on the football field for practice and had to get the team into its next drill.

That was the first time I spoke to a coach by phone while he was at practice.

Q – What's your best-feel-good story?

A – Besides Joe Brazas' remarkable comeback?

I have to go with the husband/wife coaching team that was in charge of the highly successful Jamaica High School girls' basketball program of the 1990s.

Dawn Eakle was the head coach and her husband, Barry, was the assistant. They took over a program which had four consecutive sub-.500 seasons and quickly built a mini-dynasty.

Jamaica was 118-21 during their five-year tenure from 1991-92 through 1995-96. In their final four seasons, the Cardinals were 105-11 (a 90 percent success ratio) with four regional titles, three sectional titles and one state tournament appearance.

Each of their final three teams were ranked among the top six in the state in Class 1A.

I suspect they would have coached longer, but they had a young son at home and then, in 1997, Dawn gave birth to twins, and the coaches stepped aside from the high school scene. They still got to see plenty of basketball as their children eventually played the game.

Best of all, once Barry Eakle stopped coaching, he had more free time to attend games and was a frequent traveling partner with me. It worked out well. I drove him to the destination of the game and – more often than not – he drove on the return leg so I could sit in the passenger seat with my laptop and start working on my story.

I'm not sure my colleagues ever figured out how I could return from a road game and file a story within five minutes of arriving in the office.

Q – Did you have any unique milestones?

A – In December, 2000, I reached the 300-school mark for high schools in Illinois where I covered an athletic event. I didn't have far to travel for that one. It was a basketball game at Champaign's Judah Christian.

At that point, I had a literal A-to-Z list (from Altamont to Zeigler-Royalton) and had all four directions adequately covered as well. North to south went from Belvidere to Carbondale and east to west went from Danville to Taylor Ridge.

The trip to Taylor Ridge was interesting. I was headed to Rockridge High School for a wrestling meet and must have missed a turnoff sign (pre-GPS) when suddenly I came across a sign that said, "Welcome to Iowa."

Some people spend thousands of dollars to see exotic locations. All I needed was my car and the promise of a sporting event to make the rounds in Illinois to locales such as Havana, Jamaica, Nashville, Paris and San Jose.

Not until I retired and it was too late, did I realize I had missed making a trip to Cuba (Illinois).

I went to communities where you had to stop and sample the food (Sandwich) and to places where I expected to see a fast-paced lifestyle (Rushville).

Note that I said it was the 300th high school where I had covered an event. I didn't make it inside all of the school buildings. At Braidwood Reed Custer, for example, I only made it as far as the baseball diamond and at Williamsville, I was only at the softball diamond.

After 300, I didn't keep an accurate count, but I estimated I wound up at 350 different Illinois high schools.

Q – What is the most bizarre thing you've written about?

A – There's a tie here.

The 1978 Urbana High School baseball team had two players with the same name.

I suppose if their names were Pete Smith or John Jones, it might not be so unusual.

However, these athletes were named David Halberstadt. In order to keep their exploits separated, we referred to them in print by also using their middle initials. One was David A. Halberstadt and the other was David W. Halberstadt.

Their fathers (Vernon and Ralph) were cousins.

The young baseball players were both in the same class, too, graduating in 1979.

And, speaking of the Smiths ... it took almost a quarter of a century for something to match the Halberstadts.

In the fall of 2002, Paxton-Buckley-Loda had three players named Kyle Smith on the football team. Two of them were juniors who started on varsity.

Kyle W. Smith was a running back for a team that was a regular in the state rankings. Kyle J. Smith was a linebacker.

Thanks to nicknames, coaches could quickly communicate with the proper Kyle Smith. Kyle W. Smith was known as "Smitty." Kyle J. Smith went by "K.J."

The third Kyle Smith was a sophomore, Kyle L. Smith.

To make the situation more confusing that year at PBL, there were six players overall named Smith playing football.

Q – Any embarrassing things happen to you over the years?

A – Yes, as a matter of fact.

There's a reason I've always referred to former UI volleyball head coach Mike Hebert as the most congenial and cooperative coach with whom I've dealt at any level.

I covered his teams on a regular basis for several years. In August, 1989, I set up a time to meet him after practice. He asked me to arrive at 3 p.m.

The day scheduled for the interview, I showed at Kenney Gym, where the Illini then played their home games, thinking I was early. It didn't take a brain surgeon to see that practice was about to begin.

Hebert came to where I stood and asked what he could do. It was clear there'd been a mix-up on the time. He then said that practice was starting at 3 and wouldn't be over until 5, but I had scheduled another interview for that time and couldn't return. I suggested that I call him in the evening.

"Give me five minutes," he said.

He went over, huddled with an assistant and returned moments later, bringing two folding chairs.

"I have as much time as you need," Hebert said.

We chatted for 30 minutes, and this was a year he had a nationally ranked team.

This example wasn't an exception, but an example of Hebert's genuine care and concern for others, especially those in the media.

Another memory of Illinois volleyball – far from embarrassing – was watching Barb Winsett serve every point in one game. This was when the first team to 15 points was declared the winner.

Q – Who were some of the most colorful prep athletes you've covered?

A – Great question. Here are a few: St. Joseph-Ogden's

Jennifer Brown won state discus titles from 1995-97; Danville's Chad Red was a wrestling state qualifier in 1992; Mahomet-Seymour's Brady Greene intercepted nine passes during the 2003 football season; Champaign Central's T.J. Gray was an All-Area second-teamer in basketball in 2001; Danville football quarterback Tyler Blue passed for a school record 2,394 yards in 2003 and Urbana's C.R. Black was a standout baseball catcher during the 1980s.

Q – Who were some of your favorite athletes for the various seasons?

A – There are several ideal candidates: Atwood-Hammond's Autumn Sparling was an All-Area basketball player in 1994; Villa Grove's Summer Burnett was an all-conference second-team selection in basketball in 1994; Blue Ridge's Audra May was a 20-game winner in softball in 2001; Mahomet-Seymour's Jennifer Fall was one of the area's top cross-country runners in 2004; and Westville's April Anderson was a softball standout in 1995.

Q – Are there some specific games you remember?

A – I should probably first say I remember the vast assortment of state championship teams and individuals I had the pleasure to cover, but there is one other game that stands out.

On May 3, 1995, I traveled to Rossville's Christman Park for a softball game between the hometown Bobcats and the Urbana Tigers. Urbana won 28-6. What makes the game so memorable is that the Tigers snapped a state-record 149-game losing streak that afternoon, a streak that covered 2,198 days and parts of seven years.

There was no wild celebration, however, after the victory. The Tigers were very reserved. And respectful.

"We know how it feels to lose," coach Randy Blackman said. "Why mock a team?"

Q – Can you name some area athletes and coaches you covered who had an international flair?

A –Several are prominent. Hoopeston's Merry Spain was the team's top rebounder in 1994; Danville's Justine Russian was a two-year letter winner in volleyball before graduating in 2000; Monticello's Sean German played for the Sages' 19-win team in 1990-91; Hoopeston-East Lynn's Dan French was an all-Vermilion County basketball player in both 1977 and 1978; and Centennial's Tim Irish was in charge of the Chargers' boys' soccer program from 1988-95.

Q –Who was the most inspirational athlete you covered?

A – I am sure that the most inspiring story of an athlete was that of Oakwood wrestler Justin Shaw, who graduated in 1997. He gave credence to the saying that limits shouldn't be set on what teenagers – or anyone, for that matter – can accomplish.

A wrestler, he removed an artificial leg before stepping on the mat. He had at least as much upper body strength as anyone he faced in the 135-pound weight class and was able to bench-press more than twice his weight.

Shaw was a four-year wrestling letterman, who won 20 matches as a junior and 69 for his prep varsity career. I also watched him play football in a youth league game.

Q – Did you only cover just high school, college and professional sports?

A – As a rule, yes. We certainly had many, many requests to feature junior high teams and athletes, but we had more than we could handle at the high school level, so it was a rare occasion when we featured athletes younger than high school age, unless it happened to be in an age-group swimming, tennis or golf meet.

I recall three middle school athletes that I interviewed and wrote about before they entered high school.

The first one was Jason Sempsrott. I went to Champaign's Columbia Middle School on Jan. 25, 1989 to interview the eighth-grader who was a highly touted basketball player and was averaging 26.4 points per game.

Many times, the hotshot players at younger levels don't turn out to be as spectacular as they grow older. Maybe it's because they've matured early. Maybe it's because they don't work as hard. Maybe it's because others work harder. Maybe it's because they lose interest or get burned out. Maybe they get sidelined by the academic aspect. Maybe it's for any number of other reasons.

Sempsrott was one of the exceptions. He continued to play a starring role while at Champaign Central.

He was the high school's third-leading career scorer when he graduated in 1993 and ranked fifth for points scored among anyone from Champaign-Urbana who had played basketball. He was a multi-sport star, running on a cross-country team that captured a regional title and earning a state medal in track and field for a third-place finish in the 800 meters.

Sempsrott then earned All-America accolades at South Dakota State University, where he finished top 10 in school history in both scoring and assists and was first all-time in free throw accuracy, 87.3 percent, when he graduated in 1997.

The second pre-high schooler I interviewed was Danville's Jake Strader, whom I saw play a grade school football game on Oct. 1, 1992. He was a running back for the Danville Saints, who on this Thursday night defeated Bismarck, 34-20, at Drummy Field. Strader carried the ball 13 times and rushed for 289 yards. He scored four touchdowns.

Strader enrolled at Danville High School and was a three-time All-Area placekicker. He also quarterbacked the football teams to Big 12 Conference titles as a junior and senior, helping the Vikings compile a 19-3 record in those seasons.

From there, he went on to a successful kicking career at Illinois State University, converting 32 of 54 field goal attempts in his four years with the Redbirds. He graduated in 2001 with a school record for the most extra point placements made in a season (53 in 1999) and a career (141).

While Strader was the individual standout the night I first saw him play, he wasn't the only attraction.

Saints coach Joe Anglum took a Bill Veeck or Charlie O. Finley approach to ball games, creating an environment that encouraged people to take notice.

"I knew to be successful, you couldn't just play a game," Anglum said. "You had to make it an event to give the kids something special and make them want to be a part of it."

The grade school football game I watched was broadcast on Danville's WDAN radio station. Anglum had programs for all the home games. In an era when many grade school teams played on Sunday afternoons, Anglum scheduled Thursday night games to give his athletes the chance to play under the lights.

Anglum had a unique approach to getting the game ball to the officials in the 1992 game I attended.

Four skydivers from the Illiana Skydivers Parachuting Club, jumping from 6,000 feet, landed on the field and the fourth one to reach the ground – John McClatchey, from Covington, Ind. – carried the game ball.

Of all people whose paths I crossed with as a journalist, no one was as meticulous or paid as close of attention to all details as Anglum, a 1979 Schlarman High School graduate.

For years, he has devoted much of his free time to researching varsity athletic programs from his alma mater. He has compiled a complete history for football, boys' basketball and baseball at Schlarman. He is working on volleyball and softball.

"My dad (Tom) had done a lot of research and had yearly scores," Joe Anglum said. "That was the spark to look further.

"I followed his lead and did more research. Somebody needed to document this and take it to the next level."

Joe Anglum coached the Saints for seven seasons, and in 2020 will celebrate 25 years as an English teacher at Georgetown-Ridge Farm High School.

Ironically, the third non-high schooler that I interviewed was from Schlarman Academy.

When you hear that an eighth-grader already has six scholarship offers from major colleges, it can't be ignored.

I traveled to Clinton when Anaya Peoples was an eighth-grader in 2015 to watch her Schlarman girls' basketball team capture a second consecutive elementary school association state title. Those teams didn't lose a game during either her seventh- or eighth-grade years.

She made an immediate impact at the high school level, moving into a starting role as a freshman and, ultimately, leading the Hilltoppers to back-to-back state championships as a junior and senior on teams that won 65 of 68 games. She was The News-Gazette's Area Player of the Year as a sophomore, as a junior and as a senior.

Peoples, a 2019 high school graduate and a McDonalds All-American, signed a letter of intent to continue her basketball career at Notre Dame.

Q – Besides the foggy night when you totaled a company car while working in Bloomington, were there other scary parts to any of your work days?

A – As a matter of fact, there was one other frightening event. It was April 19, 1996. That was a Friday night.

Throughout much of the 1990s, I spent time covering the auto racing action at the Vermilion County Speedway. This particular night was pretty uneventful and a number of the heat races went off without any noteworthy incidents.

Not much after 8 p.m., a decision was made to cancel the remainder of the program based on reports of possible impending weather issues. Since no rain or lightning had been observed, it was not a popular decision with many of the fans in the stands when the public address person made the announcement.

Since none of the feature races had been contested, there was no need for me to write a story, so I loaded up my car and headed for Interstate 74.

I rarely listened to the radio while driving, unless there was a ball game. I preferred to play some of my assortment of cassette tapes, usually the late, great Harry Chapin.

I was traveling westbound on I-74 and had passed the Oakwood exit and the one for Rt. 49 when I noticed up ahead what appeared to be a miles-long line of vehicles – most of which were semis – pulled to the side of the road. A few cars and vans were mixed in, too. The whole scene was highly unusual.

Having no idea about the reasons, I slowed down and kept

going for a bit. Noticing both sides of the interstate were lined with vehicles, however, it dawned on me that perhaps there was danger ahead. I found an opening between two semis and safely pulled over, roughly two miles before the Ogden exit.

My watch showed the time as 8:50 p.m. I figured when whatever issue that had caused so many to stop their travels had ended, the traffic would start moving again. I didn't notice the time that we got going again, but I am sure the wait was at least 15 minutes.

Since so many semis were taking to the road again almost simultaneously, we didn't get up to speed for several miles and I had time to scan the surroundings. I noticed a semi in bean stubble north of the interstate, several hundred yards off of the highway, but much of Ogden was darkened, so I couldn't see anything on the south side of the road.

I was curious about what had caused the delays and, after arriving home, turned on the 10 o'clock television newscast.

The lead story was about what I probably would have driven into had I not stopped when I did. An F-3 tornado had gone through parts of Ogden, damaging more than 80 structures, injuring more than a dozen people and killing one person. The death was a woman in a semi whose truck was hit as the tornado crossed the highway.

I didn't know enough to be scared at the time, sitting along the side of the road, but 60 minutes later, my hands were shaking as I was holding the television remote.

There is no way to pinpoint exactly where I would have been had I kept on driving that night, but I couldn't shake the feeling that I might have been on a collision course with the tornado.

Fred's Favorites

FAVORITE ATHLETIC
TEAMS

1. Chicago Cubs
2. University of Illinois
3. Chicago Bulls
4. Mahomet-Seymour H.S.
5. Chicago Bears
6. Chicago Blackhawks

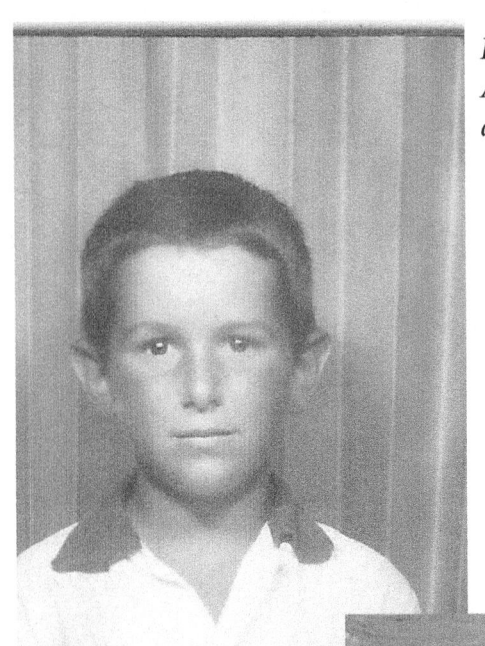

Fred Kroner,
August, 1961,
age 5 ½.

Fred Kroner standing in
the end zone at the
University of Illinois'
Memorial Stadium.

CHAPTER TWENTY-SEVEN

What do you do during down-time when you're away from the job?

For many folks, free time is devoted to watching sporting events, traveling to sporting events or participating in sporting events.

I learned decades ago that golf is absolutely no fun when you play one round every-other year and the people you are with get out on the course at least on a weekly basis. I gave away my golf clubs – which had been given to me by a former high school golf coach – and don't regret it a bit.

I wasn't raised as an outdoorsman, so hunting and fishing were never appealing. Woodworking was never a passion, either.

Watching ball games on TV – or even in person – seemed too much like work, so I sought a different outlet.

And yet, it had to be something that I enjoyed, so I started writing poetry.

I had taken several poetry writing and other rhetoric classes while at the UI – many with Jean Thompson, who was a delightful and inspiring instructor – almost finishing with enough hours for a minor, so it wasn't a reach to pursue it as an adult.

What passes as poetry – or verse – in some quarters, is far from it in my mind. I can think of many songs which I have heard on the radio with lyrics that I can't believe someone got paid to write.

Who can forget the 1969 song by Steam, which I believe had six stanzas and three of them were:

Na na na na
Na na na na
Hey hey hey
Goodbye.

My standards were different. I derived motivation from the person I consider the greatest storyteller and wordsmith of my time, singer/songwriter Harry Chapin.

I realize it's personal preference, but in my opinion, no one can tell a story like Chapin could whether it's 'Old College Avenue,' 'Corey's Coming,' 'A Better Place to Be,' 'Taxi,' 'Circle,' 'Cat's in the Cradle,' 'W-O-L-D' or 'Mr. Tanner' as well as any of the dozens of other songs that he penned so magnificently.

My goal was to tell stories within the confines of a poem, and I've spent years writing poetry in my spare time. Unlike my sports stories, which are available in the archives of any public library in Champaign or Urbana, including the UI, these were just for my personal collection and have rarely been seen by anyone else.

With guidance from my editor and muse, Dani Tietz, several dozen that are representative of my work have been selected for inclusion in this publication. It keeps with the theme of the first words I wrote when starting this book, that many people feel like they know me, but all they really know is a tiny fraction of the person I am.

Though I can, at times, be resistant to change, when Dani

suggested that I consider writing haiku, I didn't summarily dismiss the notion and – soon enough – began to embrace the challenge it presents: three total lines, five syllables in the first line, seven syllables in the second line and five in the third line.

In fact, during the past 18 months, more than four-fifths of the poetry I've written are haikus. I feel like it's still a work in progress and I'm nowhere near ready to publish a book of only poetry, but I'm comfortable sharing some special selections.

None are from the first book I wrote as a college sophomore, Asphalt Celery. That book clearly shows why I didn't earn A's in all of my rhetoric classes.

The poetry form of writing is different from any stories I've authored for newspapers. Those articles are often completed in a deadline setting and with the knowledge that one way or the other, a story will be completed in the prescribed time period.

I can't write poems on demand like I often do for newspaper articles. It doesn't work to set aside time, then isolate myself in a room with no distractions and attempt to write poetry for two hours. Occasionally, the ideas are prevalent and four or five might get completed in a day. More often than not, it's weeks – or even months – between even getting one workable idea, let alone the phrasing.

For those readers who have made it this far, there should be a better grasp of the person I am than at the outset of this manuscript.

I offer a final comment as you enter the poetry section: Happy reading!

POETRY

November 2019

Seeking perfection
Is a daily battle with
The impossible.

--

Love is a special
Word and feeling that's held
For the precious.

October 2019

Kindness goes along
With the mindset of random
Displays of smiling.

--

Heated debate always
Fuels the fire for an intense
Day of discussion.

--

Soft sounds provide a
Point of communication
For relaxation.

September 2019

Rule of thumb truth
Not pretty to be petty
Think twice and be nice.
--

The way of the world
Reservations held by two
Now there is just one.

August 2019

The forgetful man
Speaking to the firing squad
Only says, "Oh, shoot."
--

I ask, do you mind
If I focus attention
On your daily thoughts?

July 2019

My super hero
Showing unlimited powers
Erased my heartache.
--

One day, one idea
Then, one moment to savor
Now, one lifetime.

Why is it we see
The good in others before
It surfaces in us?

--

If you had a wish,
Which one would you pursue with
Reckless abandon?

--

Will this be the day
My heart skips so many beats
I no longer breathe?

--

Left on the counter
Right in line with my vision
Centerfold photo.

--

Ideas and ideals
The standards of excellence
Forming my viewpoints.

June 2019

Seeking meaning in
The words we use daily to
Express our feelings.

--

Nods of approval
Done in the blink of an eye
Will last forever.

May 2019

That time so long ago
When my to-do list was full
But life was empty.

--

Childhood memories
No matter how fleeting, seem
To bring a smile.

April 2019

Security is
The common goal of the young
Then, obscurity.

--

Heart palpitating
It's baseball season
Where is the remote?

March 2019

Good fortune is nice
Good friends are imperative
Good health is the best.

--

The smile I have
Represents total recall
Of your memory.

February 2019

Just one to wonder
About my purpose in life
And how to find it.

--

A day unlike any
And a feeling unlike any
That was yesterday.

--

The words that we say
Can encourage or dismay
And build or tear down.
--

What all would you do
For the chance to reach a dream
Without guarantees?
--

Snow melt continues
Turning streams into rivers
Assisted by my tears.

January 2019

New year and new hopes
Spectacular traditions
Are best with old friends.
--

Adversity is
Just another good chance to
Control the moment.

December 2018

People care so much
About all of your business
But not your feelings.
--

Grains of sand or tears
Impossible to say which
Number is greater.
--

Emphasize truth

Yet every night in bed
All we do is lie.
--

The goal never was
Number one in my mind
But just in your heart.
--

One lesson to learn:
Having a day off is not
At all like an off day.

November 2018

The first day of the
Rest of my life is today.
Or is it the last?
--

College memories
So far removed from my body
Seems like yesterday.

If you care enough
That is what is required
To have an impact.
--

The laughter and tears
Originate from desire
To share emotions.
--

When you break it down
Thanksgiving translates into
Thanks for your giving.

--

I would take five years
Away from the end of life
To hug mom once more.

--

Some things stay the same.
Whether I live or die
The world still revolves.

--

A specific ad:
Male seeks smiling woman
For eternity.
Each day I know you
Signals another highlight.
Not having bad days.

--

To love is to give
All the best parts of yourself
To complete someone.

--

Tragedy occurs
Usually without warning
Breaking the silence.

--

Left to my thinking
About what's right in life
I'd view the stars.

--

In my element
Surrounded by many people
But in my own world.

--

Remembering is
Easy and very pleasant
Forgetting is hard.

--

True reality check:
Good things come to those who wait
Unless you die first.

--

In your final daze
You realize it's too late
To pay attention.

--

Friendly faces belie
The evil thoughts that simmer
Below the surface.

--

The snapshot photo,
Black and white, tattered corners,
Focused memory.

Afraid of this life
Now feeling so scared to death
What else does that leave?

--

To sleep forever
In glorious contentment
Final fulfillment.

--

Insecurity

Blankets each stop that I take
Can not move forward.

September 2018

Don't want to be him.
Not the guy who knew so much
But now knows nothing.
--

My face is smiling.
That's a key part of the act.
My heart is breaking.
--

Why did I bother
To rinse away the anger
And wash out my mouth?
--

Why did I grow up
So unprepared to battle
Daily injustice?
--

Driven by hunger
And anxious to finally
Taste the sweet success.
--

You will always be
Beautiful because of
What you have inside.

--

I never want to

Experience a moment
Without your sweet smile.
--

Celebrate today.
Dance to the special music
And write your own song.
--

Reading and writing
My great lifetime pursuits
Talk about good days.
--

Face of beauty
Shining brilliant in my life
With an open mind.
--

Forget what I took
From the journey we're on
Just that I left it.
--

We try to hurry
To life's destinations
And then quickly leave.
--

I am a wonder.
At times, I also wonder
What is my purpose?
--

If you see me on
My deathbed, say it's time to
Finish my story.

August 2018

Dreams are inviting,
But often unreachable.
Life gets in the way.

--

Perfect partnership
Is one where each person
Makes contributions.

--

Daily to-do list
Now condensed to one item:
How can I help you?

--

Many tomorrows
Must come and go before we
See a better day.

July 2018

Every day I
Am hopeful tomorrow
Is a better day.

--

Always curious,
Does cloud nine ever conceal
The perfect ten?
The wind swirls your hair
Creating interlocking knots
And tangles our dreams.

--

Each day, exciting
Never knowing what is next
Even with plans made.

--

What gains have we made
When our voices override
Feelings of the heart.

--

Advice in this era
Not what I was ever told
Give it your best shot.

--

Sleepless again and
Performing one more sheep count
Thinking, I love ewe.

--

In a fake news world
Reality is unknown
While seeking the truth.

--

The answer depends
Regardless of the question
On the point of view.

--

Morning rain, wet sand
Ocean waves, break in the clouds
Solo gull attacks.

June 2018

Here I thought I meant
Something, but I learned I
Meant something else.

--

Waited my entire life
For the moment of magic
Then it disappeared.

--

Worker bee tried hard
To complete obligations
Or die while trying.

--

Burying our thoughts means
The same as burying people
For what they might think.
All my glory years
Suddenly vivid again
From decades long ago.

--

Cutting pink peonies
Catching a scent heaven sent
Highlighting my day.

--

Game time has arrived
Playing word association
The first clue is truth.

--

Wet pants from the rain
Dampens my enthusiasm for
Soaking up knowledge.

Hours drag on like weeks
Week feel like months whenever
Our time is on hold.

--

Vocabulary
Words without hesitation
Defines your friendship.

--

Solitary soul
Reading her book as I hope
She can read my mind.

--

Life is so entwined
Sliced bread never did exist
Before knives arrived.

--

My summer pursuit
Making most careful choices
Picking raspberries.

--

Buying clothes buys time
To mask the stark appearance
Of a distressed look.

--

An aptly named wife,
She was the Joy in his life
Until death arrived.

--

Quick-witted seamstress smiled
Speaking her words of wisdom:
You reap what you sew.

May 2018

Freedom to express
Is a fundamental right
Why does it feel wrong?
--

Candlelight writing
Creating vivid memories
While sparking thoughts.
--

The lens was on zoom
The moment was so fleeting
The picture was clear.
--

Cereal once again
Not exactly good for thought
But the milk is warm.

This place, your own space
Stacked neatly with memories
With no room for me.

February 2018

When I drive alone
It is not enjoyable
Because the tears flow.

January 2018

So very much alike
Faith in you like in myself
How can I go wrong?

--

Traveling to town
Hampered by slow traffic
A true writer's bloc.

--

Looking back I see
There always has been so much
To look forward to.

--

Of the words you say
The most pleasing ones to hear
Are the phrase, 'you write.'

--

You tell me what hurts
And I feel the pain myself
As my own heart breaks.

--

If given the chance
To have a complete redo
I would not be me.

--

Why expect flowers
When no one puts forth effort
To plant seeds that grow.

The Master Plan

January, 2018

As time is in the final hour, will we marvel at the power
And see the light, which beckons so bright?
When all is said, and the music is dead
When it's the end of the line, rest assured I will be fine.

We all want our stories told, so memories they will hold
When the birds soar, and it's time for the exit door
When we hear thunder, will we begin to wonder
How can it be so, where did the time go?

When we hover on the brink, what will we think?
Will we wonder what it meant, this time we spent?
Living out each day, so others can say:
He was the man who always has the plan.

Except when we look, these was an unwritten chapter in
the book.
There is still much to do, but that is nothing new.
As for my dream, it is simple it would seem
As I near the final mile, I will think of you and smile.

That Guy
January 2018

I want to be the guy
Who gives without seeking payment
Who helps without asking for assistance
Who leads without expecting followers.

I want to be the guy
Who is a friend without expectations
Who is calm without exceptions
Who loves without conditions.

I want to be the guy
Who is present without overstaying
Who shows without preaching
Who stands tall without overpowering.

I want to be the guy
Who shares without receiving
Who understands without judging
Who is thankful without insincerity.

I want to be the guy
Who has a quest without limits
Who has a vision without clouds
Who has a dream without doubters.

On Life's Journey
April 2018

Judge me, if you know me.
Criticize me, if you understand me.
Quiet me, if you see me uninformed.
Comfort me, when all else fails.

Help me, because I am hurting.
Support me, because you love me.
Guide me, because I know you can.
Trust me, because I truly care.

Appreciate me, not for my accomplishments,
But for what I try to do.
Respect me, not for my awards,
But for the example I set.

Admire me, not because I seek it,
But because I somehow deserve it.
Follow me, not because I know the way
But because the journey is worthwhile.

Listen to me, not because I have the answers
But because I yearn for solutions.
Smile for me, not out of duty,
But because of sincere affection.

Forgive me, for my mistakes.
Accept me, with my imperfections.
Protect me, from the daily cruelty.
Join me, so I don't have to do it alone.

Healing
December, 2017

If defined by actions,
Do we measure success
By the number of glories
Accumulated on our work?

If defined by dreams,
Do the vivid visions
Match the reality
That became our life?

If defined by possibilities,
Did we land in a box
That provided limits
Stopping the growth?

If defined by expectations,
Were the challenges
Met and embraced
Or lost without desire?

If defined by love,
Did we openly share
The feelings and emotions
We anticipated in return?

Words

December 2017

Three little words
I've longed to hear
Powerfully motivating
Truthfully accurate.

Three little words
Equal in length
To erase doubts
And supply inspiration.

Three little words
A sentence to pronounce
A lifetime I've waited
I'd like to believe

Three little words:
Yes
You
Can.

Everything
Christmas Eve 2017

Every day
Is an opportunity
To show kindness
That was missing.

Every person
Is an individual
Who is in need
Of something.

Every hand
Could one day
Be attached
To your wrist.

Every smile
Given freely
Is a joy
And valuable.

Every heart
Wants simply
The feeling
Of acceptance.

The Gift
2017

I try never to ask for much
Don't needs gifts and such.
Money is nice, but not the end of the line.
If I don't have it, I can live just fine.

Friends come and go
That's one fact of life I know.
Some days I live fancy free,
Others I cry until I can't see.

But if I were to sometime start a wish list
And check to make sure nothing is missed.
There's one item I could not overlook
It's as important to me as food to a cook.

It remained the same as time changed the years
And guided me through my deepest fears.
In it, I confidently say I completely trust
Knowing its presence is an absolute must.

I don't have many things I need.
No huge ego there I have to feed.
In fact, all I require once in a while
Is occasionally to see your beautiful smile.

Flowers
2016

A flower is so lucky
In a well-tended garden
Providing gorgeous beauty
For those who happen by.

Standing tall in a vase
It symbolizes a feeling
Captured for the moment
And known as love.

When it goes
The fragrance remains
The memory lingers
The feelings are alive.

The three-letter word
2012

My favorite word has three letters
And I can never get enough of it.
Morning, noon and especially at night
The time is always just right.

Since the time I was young,
And now that I have aged,
I find this wonderful word
Constantly on my mind.

Whether out of town on a trip,
Or working at the office late,
I am simply unable to escape
From the thought of this word.

It's eternally true, I must admit
That it has become a regular habit.
And one not likely to change soon
What I want, of course, is Y-O-U.

Life's Values
June 2004

Everything in your life has led to this day.
Your graduation and the time to head a new way
All that means so much will remain in your mind,
But as the future arrives, you are sure to find
The best days are truly just a step away.

Advice will freely be offered by many to you
And yet, the best motto is to yourself be true.
Don't seek out others to try and please.
Just share your joy and life will be a breeze
The world will happily embrace your presence.

So many people do not understand,
They'll donate money, but won't lift a hand.
They'll think of themselves, before others in need
You'll have a chance to make a difference, do a good deed,
Which will make you richer than any money can earn.

You will know many people in your life
Some through good times, some through strife.
When it's your turn to be judged for all that you've done
It's not important whether you achieved a little or a ton,
The telling tale will be if you were a good friend.

Mother
December 2003

In a world of uncertainty and strife
Death and taxes are still a fact of life.
Those rules are true, but there is another
You didn't get there without a mother.

They can be seen in all shapes and styles
Sometimes they frown, usually they're all smiles.
They love you if you're good or if you're bad.
They love you if you're happy or if you're sad.

A mother is one word which encompasses so much,
A shopping companion or a friend with a gentle touch.
She can act stern or tough, but she's always fair,
That's why she's a woman beyond compare.

There are millions of mothers in the world today,
But there is one about which we'd all say
No one else is as nice or as sweet
Calling her mom is a genuine treat.

The reference is made to the mother who's your own
The one whom you'd like to see made into a clone
We'll miss her now that she has gone away,
But yet, we will remember her each and every day.

Stopwatch
2002

The children play gleefully
Unaware of their surroundings
Until the moment arrives
That a parent is done working.

Suddenly the time is now
To make an impression
And with a childish plea
They beg. Stop. Watch.

Those same kids become teen-agers
And gather again on a track
Ready for another race
Down the cinder straightaway.

They look at the finish
A familiar sight appears
Each and every observer
Is holding a stopwatch.

Life reflects a child's play
Yet with one huge difference
Which is universally true
No one can freeze a moment.

As the clock keeps ticking
How many of us enjoy the time
And no matter how busy we are
How many just stop and watch?

The Road Less Traveled
October, 1999

I traveled the road and counted the miles.
I reached your house and counted the smiles.
I counted my dreams when I was away.
That's why I return here today.

I counted the kisses. I counted the tears.
I counted the laughter. I counted the fears.
It all adds up to a love I want to share.
I'll travel any distance to show how much I care.

The distance apart has been too great.
I've uncovered feelings that will not wait
I must share with you this love inside
So I got in my car and took a long ride.

The path took me directly to you
With feelings so honest, direct and true.
The gas tank is empty, but my heart is filled
With a desire so strong it makes me strong-willed.

You're It
June, 1998

I remember the games we played
Every day at every recess
To our delight and our dismay.
Tag. You're it.

I remember uneasy times in the classroom
Teacher ignoring all the raised hands
To pick her own volunteer.
Whew. You're it.

I remember when I realized
Girls are delicate and delightful
There was one reason for that feeling.
My. You're it.

As I look back on those long-lost years
So much of it is forgotten or a blur
One memory stays vivid and prominent.
Definitely. You're it.

My Life
October, 1998

My life has featured frowns, but very rarely a smile
Happiness is not a feeling I knew for a long while
Good days were the ones where I could stop crying
Bad days were the ones where my heart started lying
Telling me the worst was now in the past
When I knew the suffering was all that would last.

One day without warning or even a reason
I found my life had hit a brand-new season
I looked in the mirror and saw a smile on my face
The feeling inside was one I could never replace
I felt wanted and needed and my spirits would soar
Knowing yesterday's heartaches would return no more.

Your love has filled me and made me content
In my mind, I know you had to be heaven sent
Every day is filled with wonder, satisfaction and joy
I am deliriously happy, like a child with a new toy
You are everything that I have ever wanted
You are what I chased when I searched and hunted.

Now that I have you, it is safe to say
How you put the sunlight back in my day
How you give me the strength and courage to move ahead
How I'll take your hand and willingly be led
To the time in the future where our lives are one
And our days are filled with nothing but fun.

How My World Runs
November 1998

We're all players in life's big game
Seeking our fortune, seeking our fame.
Everyday we try and we give it our best
When it's time to put our skills to the test.

Some of us run to simply try and win.
Some of us run to escape where we've been.
Some of us run best if there's someone to chase.
Some of us run best when there's no one to face.

You want to win and I want to win, too.
Seeking success is just not anything new.
But win or lose, you know life will go on.
So prepare yourself for a new day's dawn.

The value of coaches are the lessons they teach.
"Your goals are there, but not always within reach."
The value of a friend is the support he can show
As you struggle to defeat each and every foe.

Now just in case you couldn't tell
As you prepare for this race, I wish you well
And remind you to relax as you run
Go for it hard, but try to have fun.

This Day
1996

For many, this is another day in their lives
An inconsequential one as the world turns
As they grow older, yet act young and restless
And the guiding light in their life flickers.

For you, it is a glorious day of new beginnings
A time to celebrate proud accomplishments
A moment to cherish with pride and delight
An event to remember as a crowning highlight.

The cynics will ask with a slight sneer
"What's the big deal about a graduation?
Why the fuss over getting a diploma?
How can that occasion be so memorable?"

Do they not see that this is a symbolic day?
A time to pause and reflect upon work well done.
A way to acknowledge an effort which was supreme.
And to applaud the individual who pulled off this feat.

For some, this may indeed be just another day.
For some, the World Series is just another game.
For some, Garth Brooks is just another singer.
For some, Porsches are just another vehicle.

For you, this day is more special than all others combined.
The congratulations are more deserving than at any other time.
The smiles beam larger and the hugs are more precious
As you are recognized for honors that make you unique.

For me, words can not describe the feeling in my heart.
Actions can not account for the satisfaction I feel.
Kisses can not reveal the love which I know
But this knowledge is true: I am so proud of you.

Concluding the Final Termination
1996

Forgetting is not so easy to do
After the heartache you put me through
Forgiving is also very hard
With a heart permanently scarred.

Understanding is an open phrase
Like a fire going from a simmer to a blaze
It can be easily quelled
So that inner feelings are no longer held.

Like a car without reverse
And a funeral director without a hearse
The main ingredients weren't properly mixed
A relationship started before the ties were fixed.

And now we can see it's over
Despite this four-leaf clover
There's nothing more to say
But it's a shame it ends this way.

A Runner's Good Luck
October 1992

This is the story of a cross-country race
And of a girl who had hoped for first place.
The gun sounded and off she went
To the front of the pack, she was hardly spent.

The temperatures were cool, the air was heavy.
For some, a day better spent than driving a Chevy.
But the girl moved out as fast as she could
Seeking a time that would be extremely good.

Onward she pushed, ignoring pain in her side.
As the course grew tougher, to herself she cried,
"Why me, why me? I've worked so hard."
To her surprise, an inner voice caught her off guard.

"You think you're the only one who feels so bad.
Don't get down on yourself, don't feel sad.
You can do it only if you think you can.
Remember the strategy, remember the plan."

"Treat pain as a friend, call it the price you pay.
And then let nothing stand in your way.
It seems to me that your goals are clear.
They are all within reach, all so near."

The girl knew that the voice was right.
And just up ahead, the finish line was in sight.
When the race was over, there was no pain, not a trace.
Because a first-place trophy left a smile on her face.

The Dream
August, 1983

I imagine the golden years, of being eighty-two
A simple life, of being there with you.
And a sun-swept day, taking a new bride
Then alone at night, sitting at home with pride.

You will be there to hug and there to hold
Through the summer heat and the winter cold.
I breathe a sigh of relief, together at last
Doing whatever we do and having a blast.

Life is so full of simple pleasure
The moments all ones we will treasure
Playing cards and sleeping late
Nothing about this life we hate.

Spending winters in the Florida sun
Enjoying your company and having fun
Visiting with friend after friend
Side by side until the very end.

Never again will I walk through life alone
With a heart that I've had out on loan
So that's the story of my big dream girl
Someday it would be nice to give it a whirl.

Acceptance
1982

I sit quietly and blink back the tears.
I am filled with emotion and a new set of fears.
I feel like my dreams have been crushed
And my voice forever will be hushed.

I want too much, I know I do.
You've said it before, it must be true.
Friends are just friends, lovers they're not.
So why can't I be happy with what I've got?

The best kind of friend is one who is true.
The best kind of friend of which there are few.
The best kind of friend is one with time for me.
The best kind of friend makes me happy, you see.

What I want is a friend who may one day be my mate
Someone to share life with before it's too late
Someone to whom I can talk and confide
Someone whose beauty comes from inside.

I have the dream, but I don't sleep much anymore.
I am losing this battle and I've stopped keeping score.
I sit here quietly as another tear falls from my eye.
I take a deep breath and all that comes out is a sigh.

Separate Checks
1979

Two checks are better than one, you know.
Isn't it funny how a marriage can go.
Working apart to live together.
Spending money to make life better.

Fighting the bills, fighting each other.
Learning the roles of father and mother.
Changing diapers, changing your job.
Home at night to contend with the mob.

Blending minds, uniting the spirit.
Three hurrahs and one let's hear it.
Married life is a ton of thrills.
Then it's time to pay more bills.

Two checks are better than one, you know.
But it's not hers and mine, no, no, no.
It's mine and all that overtime.
For now, forever, no other sign.

If you don't mind, I'll take what's mine.
Give you the rest and we will find
What we always should have known
How easy it is for a marriage to be blown.

Hope
(undated)

Happiness comes now in waves
Like the hand that offers a greeting
While traveling the country roads
And noticing a family on their porch.

The moments are forever memorable
Though the elapsed time is fleeting
We fondly recall highlights of the past
We optimistically anticipate the future.

And yet the life moments of this day
Are seemingly forgotten in a flash
Leaving only an unrequited desire
To be flooded by a happiness wave.

Fred's Favorites

MISCELLANEOUS
1. Favorite cartoon: The Lockhorns
2. Favorite beverage: Dr. Pepper
3. Favorite pie: Pumpkin
4. Favorite vegetable: Sweet corn (on the cob)
5. Favorite fruit: Raspberries
6. Favorite meat/fish: Shrimp

ABOUT THE AUTHOR

Mahomet native Fred Kroner's autobiography is his seventh book.

He also authored Parkland Perfection 'Be together, not the same' (2016); 'A Saucer Coming To Rest' A Half-Century of the Assembly Hall (2013); Catching Up, The Official History of the Eastern Illinois Baseball League (2010); Are You Ready? Jim Sheppard – A career announcing Illinois football and basketball (2007); Brian Cardinal: Citizen Pain (2001) and Asphalt Celery (1974).

He has written for Central Illinois newspapers for more than half a century.

From 1968-73, he wrote sports articles for weekly Mahomet Sucker State. This began while he was in junior high school.

From 1974-78, he wrote part-time as a sportswriter for the Champaign-Urbana Morning Courier, covering an area of approximately 50 high schools. This was while he was attending the University of Illinois.

From 1978-81, he wrote full-time as a sportswriter for the Bloomington Daily Pantagraph, covering an area of approximately 60 high schools.

From 1981-2015, he wrote full-time as a sportswriter for the Champaign-Urbana News-Gazette, covering an area of approximately 50 high schools. He retired as the newspaper's sports editor.

From 2015-17, he wrote for Mahomet Citizen, first as a sports columnist and then as the newspaper's editor;

From 2017-19, he has written for the online Mahomet Daily, covering both sports and news stories.

Among his numerous career achievements:

--2001, Chosen as the state of Illinois recipient of Sportswriter of the Year by the National Sportswriters and Sportscasters Association. This award goes annually to one individual per state, regardless of size of newspaper;

--2009, Inducted into the Illinois Basketball Coaches and Officials Association Hall of Fame;

--1985, Nominated for a Pulitzer Prize;

--1984, 1988, 2000, 2009, Chosen as the winner of the Newsman of the Year award for the entire state by the Illinois Wrestling Coaches and Officials Association. He was the first person to win the recognition four times. He was also a finalist with the IWCOA in 1986, 1987, 1989 and 2014;

--2008, Chosen by the Illinois Coaches Association as Softball Writer of the Year for the entire state of Illinois;

--2015, Won the Distinguished Media Award, presented annually to a person or persons from the entire state by the Illinois High School Association;

--Recognized numerous times by either The Associated Press or the Illinois Press Association for articles he wrote that were judged to be top five in state or national competitions. These awards included, but were not limited to, second place 2004; third place 1989; fourth place 1978 and fifth place, 1985;

--In 2000, he was listed in Marquis' millennium edition of Who's Who in America.

There have been numerous other behind-the-scenes activities which he did without fanfare.

-- For 25 years, through 2015, he handled selections for The News-Gazette's All-State teams in girls' basketball and volleyball;

--For 20 years, through 2014, he was one of eight media members selected by the Chicago Bears to pick a weekly High School Coach of the Week in football;

--For 20 years, was a member of The Associated Press panel that voted in the weekly state rankings for football as well as for boys' basketball and girls' basketball;

--For 19 years, he volunteered as an instructor at the Sports Media Camp for Kids, in Danville and provided transportation to three different Mahomet teen-agers in order for them to attend the week-long camp;

--In 2001, he was one three Illinois journalists to partic-ipate in the Second-Annual Sports Media Practitioner Workshop in Antigua;

Kroner has been selected for induction into two Hall of Fames for 2020. On April 25, he will be enshrined in the Illinois Wrestling Coaches and Officials Association (IWCOA) Hall of Fame.

He will also be added to the Mahomet Education Foun-dation Hall of Fame on Friday, Sept. 18, 2020 as part of a four-member class that will also include Jason Seaman, the late Leo Vitali and Janet Watkins. The ceremony will take place prior to the homecoming football game that night against Effingham.

Kroner is married to another Mahomet-Seymour High School graduate, the former Emily Moon, who is the owner and operator of Lucky Moon Pies & More, in Mahomet.

Between them, they have four children: Devin (Eliza-beth) Kroner; Sal (Shea) Belahi; Jamel Belahi and Malika

Belahi. They have seven combined grandchildren: Titus Kroner; Matthan Kroner, Larkin Kroner; Esli Kroner; Brayden Anthony; Addison Anthony and Preston Belahi.

Fred Kroner's 2009 plaque for the Illinois Basketball Coaches Association Hall of Fame.

(Above) Fred Kroner works on a story after a session of the Vermilion County basketball tournament at Danville's Palmer Arena.

INDEX

I

J

K

M

O

P

S

T

U

Y

Z

Made in the USA
Monee, IL
27 January 2020